BEST MUSIC FOR YOUNG BAND:
A SELECTIVE GUIDE
TO THE YOUNG BAND/YOUNG WIND ENSEMBLE REPERTOIRE

First Edition

BEST MUSIC

FOR

YOUNG BAND

A Selective Guide
to the Young Band/
Young Wind Ensemble Repertoire

First Edition

by Thomas L. Dvorak

Director of University Bands,
The University of Wisconsin–Milwaukee

with Cynthia Crump Taggart

Doctoral Graduate Teaching Assistant,
Temple University

and Peter Schmalz

Director of Bands,
Oshkosh West High School

edited by Bob Margolis

Manhattan Beach Music
Brooklyn, New York • 1986

Copyright ©1986 by Manhattan Beach Music

Published by Manhattan Beach Music
1595 East 46th Street
Brooklyn, New York 11234-3122

First Edition

Current printing (last digit):

10 9 8 7 6 5 4 3 2

Library of Congress Cataloging-in-Publication Data

Dvorak, Thomas L., 1941–
    Best music for young band.

    Includes indexes.
    1. Band music--Juvenile--Bibliography--Graded
lists.   2. Wind ensembles--Juvenile--Bibliography--
Graded lists.   I. Taggart, Cynthia Crump, 1957–
II. Schmalz, Peter.   III. Margolis, Bob.   IV. Title.
ML132.B3D9   1986   016.7851'25   86–12443
ISBN 0-931329-02-7 (pbk. : alk. paper)

CONTENTS

FOREWORD

Perhaps the most important task to face all conductors is the choice of the most appropriate literature. This becomes a never ending quest and is made even more difficult in the public schools due to the exorbitant time demands of a great variety of responsibilities. The selection of quality music is further complicated by the deluge of superficial publications which constantly emerge each year to attract our attention.

In this climate of artistic frustration due to the limited amount of quality musical choices, this listing by Thomas Dvorak becomes an extremely important contribution. Professor Dvorak's listing provides a vehicle through which quality choices of literature can be made with confidence. This is a singular contribution to the field of music education.

H. Robert Reynolds,
Director of University Bands,
University of Michigan, Ann Arbor.
President, College Band Directors National Association 1983-85

PREFACE

This catalogue began as a pursuit by two graduate students and myself during our days together at the University of Michigan, Ann Arbor. The early research effort and interest shown by Gary Ciepluch of Madison, Wisconsin, and William Garvey of McFarland, Wisconsin, is deeply appreciated. It is to these two fine teachers that this book is dedicated.

Several successful Wisconsin elementary/junior high school band conductors shared their personal repertoire lists, and to these conductors go a sincere thanks:

Glenn Nielsen of McFarland, Wisconsin; Gary Owens of Flint, Michigan; David Reul of Oconomowoc, Wisconsin; Larry Simons on Kenosha, Wisconsin; Scott Shuler of Rochester, New York; and Linda Dvorak of Muskego, Wisconsin.

A large number of scores were provided by music publishers throughout the United States. Because of their interest and generosity, this publication became a reality. A most heartfelt thanks to:

Alfred Publishing Company, Inc; Allaire Music Publishing; Bourne Publishing Company; Carl Fischer, Inc; E.C. Schirmer Music Company; European American Music Dist. Corp; FEMA Music Publications; Hal Leonard Publishing Corp; Manhattan Beach Music; Oxford University Press; Theodore Presser Co.; and TRN Music.

Finally, without the dedication, hard work, and expertise of my two collaborators, Cynthia Crump Taggart and Peter Schmalz, and my editor, Bob Margolis, this publication would have been difficult, if not impossible, to complete. Their insight and skills were essential to the project.

It is extremely encouraging to all of us who value the musical growth of the young that a substantial repertoire of aesthetic character exists for them. It is my hope that all conductors who share these values will continue to make this project an ongoing one as well, by informing my publisher, Manhattan Beach Music, and through them, myself, of worthy compositions that exist for younger-aged bands.

Thomas L. Dvorak,
Associate Professor; Director of University Bands,
The University of Wisconsin–Milwaukee.
February 13, 1986

TO THE READER

Best Music for Young Band: A Selective Guide to the Young Band/Young Wind Ensemble Repertoire is intended mainly for two audiences:

For the conductor of younger bands and wind ensembles, from elementary through junior high school, to moderately-easy high school level, this work will be of practical use in the field as an aid to selecting repertoire.

For teachers and students of college-level methods and wind-literature courses, this work will be useful for locating the most promising music for further study. Indeed, all musicians who have a need for a source book for grades I, II, and III band literature will find this book invaluable.

Professor Thomas L. Dvorak has spent more than six years of research, conducted at the University of Michigan, Ann Arbor, and the University of Wisconsin–Milwuakee, in preparation of the manuscript for this book. Certainly, all the works appearing herein are of the highest calibre. However, many works of equal, and perhaps even higher quality do not appear in this book. They may do so one day, or they may never do so. It is impractical, and probably impossible, to review every existing publication, and it is certain that assessing the value of music is a matter of personal judgment. Hence, readers may discover that their favorite work, whether by intent or oversight, is not included, or perhaps that a work in their personal disfavor, is. *De gustibus non est disputandum*: Concerning tastes there is no disputing. Therefore, a work that does not appear here is not necessarily bad nor good. It is just not present.

This being said, I am compelled to argue for the eminent usefulness and value of this book. Professor Dvorak's musical judgment is impeccable; his criteria for the selection of works for this book is carefully reasoned, and musically and educationally sound; his experience for the past seven years as chairman of the National Band Association Band Composition Contest is more than an impressive credential—it places him in a position to have reviewed the newest music from the band world's leading composers. And finally, any book of reviews from an authority on band literature, whether wholly agreed with or not, is of value in that it focuses attention on a few from the many thousands of available works. This book does just that, and in doing so frees the band director, teacher, or student, from the not always enjoyable chore of separating the wheat from the chaff.

Best Music for Young Band contains many *outstanding* works for young band. Some of these are virtually unknown, while others are standards or classics of the literature. It is possible that some may have gone out-of-print, or that some may now be in the process of being reprinted; most, however, are likely to be stocked by music retailers, or easily orderable. A few works are in manuscript, and thus not yet widely available. Addresses for composers of those works, and addresses for publishers (or their U.S.A. distributors) are given at the back of this book, which is followed by an index of titles.

Reviews are arranged alphabetically by composer's name within the three categories of young band music, march music, and young wind ensemble music.

Bob Margolis, Editor
Brooklyn, New York
February 4, 1986

CRITERIA FOR MUSIC SELECTION

The general rationale upon which compositions are selected is reflected in the following principles:

Compositions must exhibit a high degree of compositional craft; this, of course, is an important aspect in determining the level of aesthetic experience gained by the performers.

Compositions must contain important musical constructs necessary for the development of musicianship. Among these (not all of which need be present in any given work, of course), are: a variety of keys—major, minor, modal; a variety of meters—duple, triple, combinations, and proportional metric or graphic notation; a variety of harmonic styles, from traditional to modern; a variety of articulation styles—smooth, light, detached, legato, and variations of detachment.

Finally, compositions must exhibit an orchestration that, within the restrictions associated with each grade level, encourage musical independence both of individuals and sections. By way of explanation of this last criterion, it must be said that too much repertoire emphasizes homophonic scoring, usually with large groups of instruments playing all at once, and that this, or at least too much of this, often precludes the possibility of developing independence in young musicians. Such "safe" scorings may initially allow the band to sound better, but without some "unsafe" (i.e., transparently scored works) the musicians cannot fully develop their musicianship.

CRITERIA FOR GRADE LEVEL ASSIGNMENTS

Assigning grade levels can be tricky. Even if the most precise criteria are strictly adhered to, the resultant assignment of grade may not seem right. Music is not an exact science, hardly a science at all; hence, grading music becomes an art in itself, with experience, and "feel" of a piece being the best guides. Notwithstanding this, there are a number of guidelines that can be helpful in grading music. Outlined below are those followed in the present book. Please note that the "I, II, III" system used here represents the bottom half of a grade "I through VI" spectrum, with grade IV being challenging for high school, grade V challenging for college, and grade VI challenging for the very finest, most advanced bands. However, our interest is with the lower grades used in this book:

Grade I: Basic rhythms. Restricted ranges. Undeveloped technique. Homophonic texture. Much uniformity of rhythms throughout band. Ample doubling. Much full and half tutti scoring. Suitable for first year elementary school bands, and beginning middle school or junior high school bands. Not useful for high school bands.

Grade II: Intermediate rhythms; some syncopation; duplet and triplet rhythms. Expanding ranges. Fluent technique. Changing meters. Some independence of parts. Mature musical constructs. Suitable for second year elementary bands, and second year middle and junior high school bands. Suitable for beginning-of-the-year training works for third year middle school or junior high school bands. Also suitable for young, beginner high school bands (9th Grade) as beginning music, and mature high school bands (9th or 10th grade) as works of limited technical challenge.

Grade III: Challenging rhythms; free use of syncopation. Free use of section and solo scoring. Great independence of parts. Diverse instrumentation requirements, less use of cues and cross-cues. Some use of extreme ranges and technique. Not useful for elementary bands. Suitable for mature third year middle school or mature third year junior high bands. Suitable as challenging material for first-year (both 9th and 10th Grade) high school bands, or slightly challenging material for mature high school bands (both 9th and 10th grade). Also suitable as beginning-of-the-year easy training material for mature (11th and 12th grade) high school bands.

AN INVITATION

The publisher would like to invite composers and publishers to submit band sets with cassette tapes (or full scores with cassette tapes) for consideration for inclusion in supplements and/or revisions of BEST MUSIC FOR YOUNG BAND. All such submissions are considered to be review copies and become the property of Manhattan Beach Music.

Band directors or other persons knowing of works that would merit inclusion in BEST MUSIC FOR YOUNG BAND are urged to write to us, identifying such works by their composer, title, and publisher. In the case of out-of-print or manuscript works, the loan of a score and tape would be appreciated.

All correspondence and submissions should be directed to:

The Editors,
BEST MUSIC FOR YOUNG BAND,
c/o Manhattan Beach Music,
1595 East 46th Street,
Brooklyn, New York 11234-3122, U.S.A.

PART I: CONCERT/FESTIVAL WORKS FOR YOUNG BAND

Hawley Ades: *Spiritual Festival*
Grade III   9:30   Shawnee Press

This setting of nine spirituals exhibits rhythmic vitality and musical sensitivity. Syncopations abound, so good reading skills will be necessary if the music is to retain its liveliness. In addition, homophonic scoring, solo lines, brass quartet and recitative are all to be found. This is good folk music, skillfully arranged, refreshing and musical.

Samuel Adler: *An American Duo*
Grade II   4:14   Boosey & Hawkes

This two-movement work is based upon the old American hymns, "Canaan" and "The Bennington Rifleman". Both tunes receive a traditional harmonic and rhythmic treatment. There is a wonderful, singing quality to this music, with a spirited American exuberance. No pitfalls need be overcome as this music lies well within the technical grasp of younger musicians.

Samuel Adler: *A Little Night and Day Music*
Grade III   7:00   Carl Fischer

The wind band music of Samuel Adler is characterized by superb craftsmanship, although much of his music has been too difficult for young players. Here, however, is an opportunity to engage in a wonderful Adler contemporary score, with its characteristic color, texture, density, and idiomatic thought. The composer uses changing meters (3/4, 4/4, 3/4), major/minor harmonies, and a tone row in this work. The "Night Music" is sostenuto; the "Day Music," rhythmically intense. All wind parts are demanding, the trumpets more so; the extensive percussion writing, imaginative. This is a piece for only the most mature bands.

Samuel Adler: *Merrymakers*
Grade II   3:30   Ludwig Music Publishing

This single-movement work is in the form of a miniature French Overture with characteristically dotted rhythms. Beginning with a slow twenty-measure introduction (quarter note equals 52), the piece unfolds into a livelier section (quarter note equals 132). Although many of the technical demands can be met by less mature players, the composition will stretch the musical sensitivity of the musicians through unison playing, rapid trilling, execution of grace notes, occasional changing meters (3/4, 2/4) and dynamics. Percussion requirements are minimal. The wind writing is idiomatic.

Hugh Aitken: *Four Quiet Pieces*
Grade II   3:00   Elkan-Vogel

Although this piece is short in duration, it is long in musical charm and character. Technical demands are quite modest, especially in the woodwinds and lower brass. Frequent solos for flute, clarinet, trumpet, and horn are called for, but the solo demands are brief, and certainly not excessive. Although this piece has all the characteristics of similar divertissements, its major strengths are simple thought with an engaging warmth and charm.

Toshio Akiyama: *Japanese Songs for Band*
Grade II   5:45   TOA Music

Employing a number of Japanese folk songs as the melodic fabric of this piece, the composer has produced an attractive and unusual score for band. Several interesting things are called for, including the singing and chanting of basic duple patterns. The simple nature of the writing should make this piece relatively easy to learn and play.

James Andrews: *Hill Songs*
Grade II   4:30   Shawnee Press

Folk-like melodies characterize this charming setting in three distinct sections (*fast, slow, fast*). The outer, quicker sections must be crisply articulated, with careful attention given to accents and syncopations. The middle section has a sensitive, legato nature. This music has the simple nature and charm of folk music; its careful scoring allows youngsters easy access to its content.

Stan Applebaum: *Irish Suite*
Grade III   4:25   European American Music

This tuneful 6/8 suite is not based upon Irish folk melodies, though 'tis Irish through and through. The first movement is an extroverted nautical ditty; the second movement possesses an all is quiet on the quay tranquility, and lovely solos for oboe, clarinet, trumpet, and alto saxophone. Alto and bass clarinet are active. The last movement, a rollicking change in mood, has the bright sound of a gay holiday. Winds get to stamp feet.

Stan Applebaum: *Voices of Kaluga*
Grade II 3:30 European American Music

This sustained, legato piece is based upon what the composer calls the "Russian style." Melodically, the piece is built around a simple motif and is woven together by brief runs. There are beautiful sonorities as the motif is presented in chorale form by the brass. There are no solos, and a young ensemble with good, developing young players can benefit from the sustained legato sonorities and long phrases. This is beautiful music, well-suited to the needs of the young band.

Thoinot Arbeau/Bob Margolis: *Belle Qui Tiens Ma Vie*
Grade I 2:45 Manhattan Beach Music

This beautiful and stately pavane comes from an important 16th century treatise on dancing, *Orchesographie*, by Thoinot Arbeau. The major challenge here is to allow the music to unfold at quarter note equals 82 while maintaining a legato, sostenuto, full sound. There is no "flash and crash" in this score, and therefore it may seem deceptively easy. The composer has provided an exceptional set of rehearsal and program notes as well as a facsimile of the original 16th-century song. This is music designed for young players, emphasizing soft, sustained, cantabile musicianship. The scholarly care and the edition itself is unequalled in the repertoire.

J.S. Bach/Francis Caviani: *Fugue 22*
Grade II 2:20 Kendor Music

This fugue is taken from Bach's *Well Tempered Clavier*. Because of its highly polyphonic nature, it is an excellent introduction into fugal form. Although in Bb minor, technical difficulties are minimal, with easy rhythms and gracefully-shaped lines. The real challenge of this piece is putting individual lines together in a balanced and satisfying manner. Players will need to develop a strong sense of musical independence to enjoy its value.

J.S. Bach/Bob Margolis: *Festival Prelude*
Grade III 3:00 Manhattan Beach Music

This music is familiar to keyboard players as the C Major Prelude (BWV 933) from Bach's *Six Little Preludes for Beginners*. This arrangement for young band is musically striking and fresh in that the ornamentation and Baroque sensitivity have been recaptured for a much larger medium. The execution of musical style (articulation), tempo, and dynamic contrast are the key watchwords in this score; however, because of the wise key selection (Bb Major) young musicians will find the time to place their efforts in the correct place. Although the scoring is good, the ensemble must have good players on horn, and the timpanist must be sensitive and able to capture the solo drama required.

Bela Bartok/Philip Gordon: *From "Children's Album"*
Grade I 2:10 Elkan-Vogel

While the technical demands of these two short pieces ("Magic Game" and "A Merry Chase") are limited, stylistically and musically there is much for the very young ensemble to learn. The first song, "Magic Game," is in *ABA* form with a legato *A* section and a contrasting, more crisply articulated *B* section. The second song, "A Merry Chase," is in d minor, and is a lively canon between woodwinds and brass. The piece is excellently scored and its content gives the very early ensemble an exposure to important instrumental music concepts.

Bela Bartok/Philip Gordon: *Three Hungarian Songs*
Grade II 2:16 Bourne Publishing

These three short contrasting songs exhibit much charm and flavor. Instrumentation is well suited to Grade II, and only a horn solo in the second movement presents technical problems. The music will demand light and crisp articulations, with an engaging sense of folk song spirit.

Bela Bartok/William Schaefer: *Four Sketches*
  from *Pieces for Children*
Grade II 4:30 Elkan-Vogel

This four-movement suite (*Prelude, Serenade, Dance,* and *Finale*) is rich in humor. Younger players ready for syncopation, dotted rhythms, and changing meters (2/4, 3/4), will be challenged by this piece. The Bartok musicianship has been excellently retained in this arrangement. A worthwhile piece for teaching musical concepts.

Warren Benson: *Ginger Marmalade*
Grade III 3:00 Carl Fischer

Warren Benson's compositional craft is well-known to wind conductors of more advanced levels, and this commission now brings his skills and insights to younger bands. The piece is a double canon, light in texture, emphasizing crisply articulated accents and staccatos. The percussion writing is for nonkeyboard instruments, and moments of hand clapping and heel rapping provide some interesting timbres. The main teaching problem in this music will be maintaining a steady, consistent tempo with only very subtle shifts of dynamics and line. Musical independence and control, without overblowing, are keys in the performance.

15

Warren Benson: *Night Song*
Grade III 6:30 Chappell

There is emotional strength in this music, and to achieve its import conductors and players must be capable of sustaining long lines, maintaining dynamic control, and achieving proper blend and balance. Trumpet solos of sostenuto quality are asked for, but other instrumentation requirements are modest. The issue here is control and patience.

Joel Blahnik: *Invention No. 1*
Grade III 5:30 E.C. Kerby

A short flute solo begins this piece in minor mode, based on a simple lyric theme. The invention extends to some rather involved contrapuntal writing that demands careful listening, thus providing ample opportunity for teaching concepts of canon and hocket. Players are often required to play fragmented passages, which encourages attentive playing and a sense of individual responsibility. The contrast between light and lyrical sections and a powerful chorale with intense polyphonic passages is especially effective. The percussion writing includes some standard repetitive patterns in addition to more delicate parts for suspended cymbal and finger cymbals. Although the engraving is beautiful, staffless, blank measures are used when instruments are not playing; such measures are aligned by dotted lines that extend vertically through the score.

Joel Blahnik: *Invention No. 2*
Grade III 7:30 Joel Blahnik, manuscript

This is an interesting set of variations on a simple passacaglia theme, which has a strong appeal to young players. Care has been taken to let the variations unfold with changes in tonality, meter, tempo, and mood, which creates a pleasing sense of variety while providing continuity through the monothematic nature of passacaglia. This is excellent musical material for teaching musical independence, and yet by all measures a piece worthy of concert programming.

Henry Brant: *American Debate*
Grade III 4:20 Carl Fischer

This is an antiphonal overture, and the composer's intentions are such that unless two bands are utilized (one on stage and the other at the back of the hall), the piece should not be attempted. The effect of this spatial music may be that of an oral debate with one group playing in triple meter against the other in duple. The piece begins as a ''question-and-answer'' between the two ensembles, but as the music grows, the ensembles lengthen their playing and eventually join in a very effective statement of purpose. The piece is well written and well scored, and is most deserving of consideration for performance by the strongest of band programs.

Heskel Brisman: *The Gift to be Simple*
Grade II 2:45 Elkan-Vogel

Although this arrangement of the famous American Shaker hymn is limited to simple elaboration of the tune, it is a good way of introducing this famous melody. The tune is set in march style with no variation in tempo. The arranger makes use of triangle and tambourine in addition to snare drum and cymbals, adding variety to the percussion writing. Short canonic passages add contrast to an otherwise straightforward treatment of this hymn tune.

Heskel Brisman: *The Spinner's Wedding*
Grade III 1:25 Elkan-Vogel

Only the high ranges for trumpet and horn and a repetitive rhythmic structure keep this piece from being Grade II. The form is simple, with three statements of the tune (an English folk song of the textile mills of Dundee) and a bridge separating the second from the third statement. The piece is short; only the rhythmic figurations should require lengthy rehearsal time. This music is tasty and should be well-received by younger players.

Heskel Brisman: *Uganda Lullaby*
Grade III 1:45 Elkan-Vogel

This piece is one of the most popular folk songs from East-Central Africa. The tune is based upon the alternation of contrasting meters (6/8, 5/8, 6/8, 5/8, 6/8, 7/8, etc.) over an aria-like melody. The tempo is marked *Andante con moto e dolce*. Since technical problems and instrumentation requirements are minimal, the performance problems unique to this music will lie with the asymmetrical meters. The work should prove to be an invaluable resource as an introduction to the music of non-Western cultures.

Timothy Broege: *The Headless Horseman*
Grade II 1:30 Allaire Music Publishing

The strengths of this score are interesting percussion parts, creative orchestration, and a sense of drama. Players may at first resist the stylistic constructs, but this interesting programmatic piece will most assuredly become a favorite. Trombone glissandi and frequent meter changes (4/4, 6/4, 2/4) are essential to the performance of this music.

Timothy Broege: *Rhythm Machine*
Grade II   4:20   Bourne Publishing

The title of this piece seems to announce a composition of a "driving" rhythmic continuum, but such is not the case. Rather, a cleverly constructed rondo, utilizing the various melodic solo and tutti sections of the band, forms the musical basis of this work. Ample doublings make this music very playable by younger bands. With the exception of an eight-measure lyric trumpet solo, the music places limited technical demands upon the players. Percussion writing is ideally suited to young players: cymbals, snare drum, bass drum, tambourine, wood block, and timpani.

Timothy Broege: *Sinfonia VI*
Grade III   6:00   Manhattan Beach Music

This four-movement work (*Andante, Allegretto, Andante, Allegro*) emphasizes a very clear, transparent aesthetic in which subtle taste must prevail; players must therefore exercise control and independence throughout. The most important instrumentation needs can be found in the clarinets, solo baritone and percussion section. Frequent meter shifts from (4/4, 3/8/ 4/4) and (5/4, 4/4, 5/4) present significant rhythmic learning, but the overall rhythmic framework should be easily assimilated by students. Like *Sinfonia II* by the same composer, *Sinfonia VI* must be considered a major work for younger bands.

Timothy Broege: *Streets and Inroads: Fantasy for Winds and Percussion*
Grade II   3:20   Allaire Music Publishing

Eleven "avant-garde" notational symbols are clearly presented in the score and parts. The music's formal, aleatoric structure is in four various sections: *A B C* and *Interlude*, with two *Codas*. The piece provides another avenue for the aural and visual experience inherent in contemporary music.

Timothy Broege: *Three Pieces for American Band Set No. 2*
Grade III   6:00   Bourne Publishing

This set of pieces, based upon musical forms from the *Fitzwilliam Virginal Book*, begins with "Fanfare: The Jewel in the Grass;" followed by "Pavane to a Ground: The Queen in the Lake;" ending with "Fantasia: The Door in the Tree." Within the tonal and harmonic framework of D major, d minor, using seventh and ninth chords, those early forms take on a musical air admirably suited to today's expressive wind band. The score calls for a well-balanced instrumentation with a variety of percussion instruments. The piece was commissioned for a junior high band, and therefore places realistic musical and technical demands upon the players. This imaginative work is of uncompromising value to younger bands.

Anton Bruckner/Jeffrey Bishop: *Three Little Pieces*
Grade III   3:30   Oxford University Press

Music of one of the great composers of the Romantic period is made available to junior high school bands in this transcription. The gigantic scope of Bruckner's symphonies is not to be found here, however, as this is a collection of three pieces originally written as piano duets. Students will benefit from careful study of this music, especially the final piece, which demands powerful sostenuto playing at a slow tempo. Technically, there are few challenges other than occasional high passages for trumpets. Musically, there is a gold mine of opportunity for the study of Bruckner's style and musical thought.

William Byrd/Philip Gordon: *Pavana and March*
Grade I   2:00   Theodore Presser

Byrd's elegance and purity comes to life for even the youngest of wind players in this score. Through the masterful scoring of Philip Gordon, younger players have the opportunity to be sensitive and expressive. The full tutti scoring should present little technical or rhythmic challenge. The greatest concern is to play with the same style and depth of feeling that is associated with Byrd's more difficult wind music.

John Cacavas: *Choralia – Fanfare*
Grade II   2:15   Belwin-Mills Publishing

This two-movement composition presents styles which are common to the young band genre. The *Choralia* varies tone color and uses non-triadic harmonies, while large sonorities, sixteenth note figures, changing meters and a driving percussion characterize the *Fanfare*, creating an exciting and climactic final movement. This is music that is well scored and well conceived for the younger band.

John Cacavas: *Rhapsodic Essay*
Grade II   2:50   Carl Fischer

This program piece is simple in both character and conception. It is in *ABA* form, with the *A* section being massive and very stately. The contrasting *B* section is slower and more lyrical. The challenge of performing this work arrives when conductors strive for proper balance and phrasing. When performed with musicianship, *Rhapsodic Essay* can be challenging and musically pleasing.

John Cacavas: *Symphonic Prelude*
Grade III 3:30 Carl Fischer

This prelude, in *ABA* form, provides an excellent medium for a young band to develop and display a rich ensemble sound. Full tutti scoring provides a feeling of safety for young performers, enabling them to focus their attention on dynamics, articulations and balance. Sustained legato lines in the middle section require group sensitivity from all woodwinds, while heavily-accented brass chords in the opening and closing section call for mature sounds. This is an appealing piece suitable for any concert programming needs.

Charles Cardona: *Three Short Pieces*
Grade III 5:00 Shawnee Press

A single theme with subsequent development forms the musical fabric in each of the three movements of this score. Each movement has a different character, ranging from the light and subtle, to heavier sostenuto, to refreshing lyrical thought, and finally to rhythmic dance with strong dynamic contrasts. Short solos for oboe, bassoon, piccolo, trumpet, and baritone are a significant part of this music. All solos and tutti scoring are reasonable, however, and easily within the grasp of Grade III musicians.

Charles Carter: *Overture for Winds*
Grade III 4:00 Bourne Publishing

This band classic has become a favorite of many conductors. Traditionally triadic and tuneful, the music is set in *ABA* form with a somewhat fanciful and developmental treatment of the *A* section. The key centers do not go beyond three flats. Consequently, younger musicians may be more able to focus upon the technique and rhythmic vitality needed to bring this music to life. Students and audiences alike should enjoy this rather listenable band music.

Charles Carter: *Polyphonic Suite*
Grade II 3:40 Ludwig Music Publishing

This original composition utilizes three traditional vocal forms (motet, chorale, and madrigal) in a very sensitive setting for the band. Specific notes concerning the historical background and performance are provided in the score. A performance will require considerable independence because of the polyphonic and imitative nature of the music. This piece is an invaluable addition to the repertoire; it provides the conductor with ample opportunity to involve his students in comprehensive musicianship.

John Caruso: *Short Prelude With Perspectives*
Grade II 4:00 C.L. Barnhouse

This piece is built upon variations of a warm, expressive prelude, with an "Erik Satie-like" harmonic style. The contrasting *Allegro* variation requires a light, separated style of articulation from all players. Rhythmic patterns are not difficult, with some fairly simple syncopations. The work is well-scored, and there are no obvious pitfalls to overcome. This exceptional music should be included in the experience of young musicians.

Carlos Chavez: *Zandunga Serenade*
Grade III 3:30 Carl Fischer

The celebrated composer, Carlos Chavez, has given the younger band a refreshing lament, a *Serenade* that suggests, as the program notes state, the effect of "tropical nights, the sound of trees in the light wind, with distant, plaintive-like chants in the background." This 6/8 time setting, with dotted quarter note equals 50, requires players to perform with extreme sensitivity, control, and flexible technique. No unusual instrumentation is called for; however, strength in the first trumpet, horns, baritone, and percussion will greatly enhance the rehearsal momentum. Musicians have come to admire the music of Chavez, and this work is new, somehow different from his other pieces, yet bearing his creative trademark.

James Curnow: *Fanfare Prelude on "Lancashire"*
Grade III 2:15 Jenson Publications

Using the traditional church hymn, "Lead On O King Eternal," the skillful James Curnow has given the mature young band a powerful, fanfare-like piece, quite fitting as an opening selection in concert programming. This is not an easy score, and mature brass players with evenly-matched technical skills are called upon heavily. There are important percussion parts as well, which include a mallet part that adds substantially to the already brilliant sound of the woodwinds. The opening key of Db Major may present some initial difficulties; however, the primary challenge will lie with the strength needed to perform the more powerful aspects of the piece.

M.L. Daniels: *Concordium*
Grade II 3:20 Warner Brothers Music

The musical value of *Concordium* lies in the beautifully conceived chaconne, a building of variations over a harmonic progression established in the opening seven measures. Because of the polyphonic writing, players must assume a good amount of musical independence. Although a fluent technique is necessary, the main performance problem will be steady, consistent tempo and expressive control of sound. This music is well-conceived for its medium and age of performer.

M.L. Daniels: *Crusader's Theme*
Grade II   3:45   TRN Music

This setting of "God of Our Fathers" will challenge the younger bands with its demands for long, sustained phrases at a moderately slow tempo. This arrangement is traditional in concept, including modest counter-melodies, fanfare figuration, and percussion ostinato. The piece includes some sparsely-scored sections, thereby requiring a degree of musical independence from the players. This is good teaching material; it will aid in the development of a smooth, articulated legato style.

Carroll DeCamp: *Shenandoah*
Grade II   2:15   Studio P/R

This well-known folk tune is set for the young wind band in a manner that emphasizes rich sonorities and sensitive lyricism. The piece begs for a warm, free musical handling. Once the young musicians have accomplished the long sustained phrases with the inherent soft-legato tonguing, the tonal movement and harmonic growth should provide them with a uniquely rich and rewarding musical experience.

Elliot Del Borgo: *Adagio for Winds*
Grade III   4:00   Shawnee Press

Since there is little Romantic music in the original band repertoire that is approachable by young band, acquaintance with that style has been limited to arrangements and transcriptions. *Adagio for Winds* is a piece of original music by a contemporary composer that is solidly within the Romantic tradition, particularly as regards harmonic design and sensitivity of lyricism. The presence of numerous accidentals and a need for rubato, subtle articulation, and sostenuto make performance of this work decidedly more difficult than first appearances might suggest, but the rewards should be well worth the effort for players and conductor.

Norman Dello Joio: *Caccia*
Grade III   2:30   Edward B. Marks Music

This piece is based upon the style of the *caccia*, a canonic composition for two equal voices. With its rapid "fanfare-type" rhythmic and melodic imitation, and ninth, eleventh, and thirteenth chord harmonies, the music has an energetic and exciting sound. With the exception of a first cornet range to high A, technical requirements are not extreme. The piece is an important contribution to the growing aesthetic repertoire for young bands.

Norman Dello Joio: *The Dancing Sergeant*
Grade III   Edward B. Marks Music

Hardly more than a minute in length, this animated piece is "high energy" from beginning to end, and the composer's skills in orchestration are obvious throughout. Dello Joio works his rhythmic motifs equally between woodwinds, brass, and percussion. Written in 6/8 time, the primary teaching problem will be eighth note duplets that occur throughout the work. All wind players must be capable of clean, rapid articulation; the horns must also be capable of legato, cantabile playing during the middle section of the piece. All in all, a "little gem" for young bands.

Norman Dello Joio: *Scenes from the Louvre*
Grade III   10:00   Edward B. Marks Music

This five-movement work of contrasting *slow, fast, fast, slow,* and *fast* movements captures the spirit of the Louvre's development during the Renaissance. The thematic material is based upon melodies of that era. The technical demands are extreme throughout the music: The trumpet, horn, and trombone scoring provide such technical and range difficulty that, realistically, only movements I, II and IV are playable by Grade III level bands. This composition, a series of musically sensitive "gallery settings," is scored with mastery, and certainly rates as a significant piece of music for our medium.

William Duckworth: *The Sleepy Hollow Elementary School Band*
Grade III   6:00   Merion Publishers

Although the title may seem to imply a composition for elementary band of limited skill, such is not the case. Four brief sections played without pause form the framework of this aleatoric sound piece. The piece, in graphic and proportional notation, offers young players with developing technique an opportunity to experience new notational symbols and new sounds. The instrumentation needs are flexible, ranging from eleven to seventy players.

W. Duncombe/Walter Finlayson: *Early English Suite*
Grade II   7:50   Boosey & Hawkes

This four-movement suite requires only a modest technique, thereby allowing students to develop other aspects of their musicianship. Percussion writing is sparse, and should present little challenge. The music provides rhythmic training in both 3/4 and 6/8, and students will learn to develop stylistic concepts such as light, musically sensitive playing. In the second movement, balance between the legato melody and sustained chordal accompaniment may present difficulties.

Donald Erb: *Space Music*
Grade III 3:00   Mercury Music

The primary musical thought in *Space Music* is the evocation of a "world of quiet mystery" through the coloristic and technical aspects of the band. The texture is lively and surprising. Brief chromatic motifs are varied melodically and harmonically during the *ABA* structural organization, and rhythmic patterns "mesh to create an open, free time continuum." The music is scored using conventional notation. Strong, mature brass playing is a must because players are required to flutter-tongue; the trumpets are asked to shake; tessitura in first Bb cornet is rather high. The brass players also get to hiss through the mouthpiece. Occasional range problems do exist for clarinets, and at one point, the first clarinet is required to play its highest written "g." The percussion writing is imaginative and requires skillful mallet players. There is a part for piano, played mainly on the strings with a pop bottle (dragged up and down a string), and also played with the fists striking the strings, and hand strumming them. Although this music has certain technical requirements normally associated with Grade IV repertoire, quality Grade III bands can bring this score to reality because most of it is within their technical grasp. This work is sure to attract attention, and educationally, to broaden the experience of the players.

Donald Erb: *Stargazing*
Grade III 3:00   Merion Music

There are three movements in this unusual, partially aleatoric work for band. The first movement, *The Stars Come Out*, is written in proportional notation: The staccato pitches appear as black noteheads; knowing when to play the notes requires the player to make a visual judgment as to their horizontal placement within each measure. (The measures are ten seconds in duration.) This produces an unmeasured, but not entirely random effect. As the "stars come out" the notes (stars) get closer together, thereby increasing the density of the texture. This movement might well be played by Grade II or I bands as well. *Comets, Meteors, Shooting Stars* is in 4/4 meter and standard notation. There are many sixteenth-note chromatic scales at quarter note equals 120, requiring some stretch of normal Grade III technique. *The Surface of the Sun* (in 2/4 meter) features extended woodwind trills against brass flutter-tongue clusters and flaringly bubbly percussion; hot indeed! Ranges, technical problems, and instrumentation requirements are well suited to well-skilled young players. There is an electronic tape-recorded part, which is integral to the work.

Frank Erickson: *Air for Band*
Grade II 3:00   Bourne Publishing

If there is a piece that deserves to be called a *classic* in the beginning band repertoire, this is it. There is a wonderful melodic sense in the music, combined with graceful harmonic movement and skillful contrapuntal writing. All the wind players will enjoy their melodic lines. A long-time favorite of conductors, this piece is essential for developing the musical sensitivity of younger players.

Frank Erickson: *Balladair*
3:20 Grade II   Bourne Publishing

This lyrical and smooth, flowing ballad, with its traditional parallel triadic harmonic structure, is a good piece for developing a sonorous band sound and expressive melodic playing. There are no difficult technical or rhythmic problems, and even a smaller ensemble can achieve a satisfying, rich band sound.

Frank Erickson: *Dorian Festival*
Grade II 3:00   Summitt Publications

A contemporary flavor predominates in this overture-like piece. The music provides an excellent opportunity for teaching modality since the basic harmonic fabric is Dorian throughout. Because the technical demands and overall musical independence requirements are not exhaustive, podium time may be used to broaden the students' aural understanding and skills concerning modality, articulation, balance, and blend.

Frank Erickson: *Mexican Folk Festival*
Grade III 5:30   Summitt Publications

This colorful and festive piece summons images of a Mexican celebration with its syncopations, pointed rhythmic ostinatos, unusual percussion effects and generally sensitive harmonic structure. Frequent meter shifts (3/4, 2/4, 4/4, 3/4) will provide musical challenges to the ensemble. Rehearsal pacing and practice momentum should be self-motivated because of the general "playability" of the music itself.

Frank Erickson: *Rondo Royale*
Grade I 3:45   Summitt Publications

An example of rondo form blended with a variety of musical styles and melodic lyricism, this piece exhibits a refreshing musical clarity for young bands. Ranges are reasonable, and only modest technique is required to perform the piece, which can be played at the very early stages of instrumental instruction.

Frank Erickson: *Sinfonia for Winds*
Grade III 5:30 Summitt Publications

An opening brass fanfare followed by woodwind flourishes sets the stage. Frequent meter changes (2/4, 3/4, 4/4, 5/4), interchanges between triplets and duplets, and a fast tempo present constant rhythmic challenges. For much of this piece the brass and woodwinds function separately, although several tutti sections are interspersed throughout. While the main challenge is rhythmic, many of the melodies are lyrical and require developed legato playing in addition to sharply articulated styles. Although this work may require extensive rehearsal time, the musical gains should be rewarding.

Walter Finlayson: *Little Prelude*
Grade II 2:00 Boosey & Hawkes

This piece provides younger musicians with the opportunity to perform in a legato and sensitive style. Subtle dynamic shifts and ''romantic'' chordal harmonies convey a rich musical sensitivity. Playing ranges and tonal and rhythmic constructs are within easy grasp of younger instrumentalists.

Leland Forsblad: *Cantus Brevis*
Grade II 3:30 Elkan-Vogel

The espressivo nature of this music is enhanced by a warm, free, and sensitive interpretation. The key center is F Major, and the subtle shifts in harmonic and melodic direction make the piece an enjoyable listening experience. For younger players who can perform with sensitivity and restraint, this ''gem'' of simple lyricism is a must.

Arthur Frackenpohl: *Quintagon (5 Pieces for Band)*
Grade III 8:00 Elkan-Vogel

This is a most versatile piece for band, giving the creative wind conductor many programming options. The first movement, *Fanfare*, is a statement for brass and percussion only, and would serve well as a concert-opener. The second movement, *Lullaby*, is for woodwinds alone, and may also be performed separately. The next movements, *Canon*, *Dirge*, and *Rondo* are scored for full band. This is good music by one of America's fine composers. The piece is well-suited to the musical and programming needs of young band programs. .

Romulus Franceschini: *Prelude and Celebration*
Grade II 3:30 Elkan-Vogel

The composer's extensive use of phrygian harmonies gives the music an almost liturgical flavor. The opening prelude is based upon a flowing melody in a setting often poignantly dissonant. The contrasting closing section of the piece introduces a marcato theme over a harmonic base of parallel triads, and breaks a steady flow of duple meter with an occasional 3/4 meter.

Johann Jacob Froberger/Andrew Balent: *Cappricio*
Grade II 4:40 Bourne Publishing

This beautiful transcription of the Froberger C Major Cappricio is rich in Baroque chromaticism and polyphony. Instrumentation requirements are within the grasp of younger bands, although a good low brass section is required to bring this music to life.

James Froseth: *The First Individualized Concert Collection*
Grade I and II various durations G.I.A. Publications

This is a collection of sixteen pieces (in 2/4, 3/4, 4/4, and 6/8 time), each written in a way to allow simultaneous performance at various levels of difficulty by any number of players, with optional piano accompaniment. Students of varying proficiency can choose their level of technical difficulty, thereby avoiding the frustration caused by a pace that is either too slow or too quick. Concepts of tonality, phrasing, tempo, and musical style can be developed through the singing voice because the text is provided in the (mostly folk) songs. This collection is excellent instructional material as well as concert programming music for the youngest of players.

James Froseth and Andrew Balent:
Studies in Musical Literacy for Concert Band

Grade II various durations G.I.A. Publications

For conductors searching for teaching/performance music in 6/8 time, this text is a must. Both rhythmic and performance skills are taught by the written instructions/etudes; skills thus developed are utilized in playing the arrangements.

David Gillingham: *Intrada Jubilante*
Grade III 3:20 David Gillingham, manuscript

Written by the 1981 NBA/DeMoulin Band Composition Contest Winner, this march-like intrada is an exciting, high-energy piece. A well-defined sonatina form with two contrasting themes constitutes the basic design of the piece. The opening theme places a premium upon the flutes, clarinets, and cornets, while the second more expressive theme emphasizes saxophones, horns, and baritones. Although solo playing is not an issue here, the music places strong demands upon the cornet section. A continuous but rather straightforward snare drum drives the music from beginning to end. Frequent meter changes (4/4, 3/4, 5/4, 4/4) will require individual attention and careful rehearsal time. The piece is in all ways practical, rich in sound, and sensitive to the playing abilities of developing young players.

Stuart Glazer: *Modal Dance*
Grade III 3:15 C.L. Barnhouse

Many characteristics of this concert overture are quite traditional: *ABA* form (with *fast, slow, fast* tempi), parallel triadic harmony, and question and answer melodic formulas based on syncopated rhythms. It is set apart from the rest by its modal character and some interesting counterpoint. The rhythmic drive and harmonic solidity of the piece is captivating. Rhythmic problems in the slow section (particularly the triplet over two beats) will demand careful attention, as will balance between, and within, sections.

Philip Gordon: *American Frontier*
Grade I 3:20 Elkan-Vogel

As the title might suggest, this piece is based upon several well-known American folk songs. Beginning with "Aurore Bradaire," the piece winds its way through "Goodbye Old Paint" and "Skip to My Lou." This enjoyable folk material, scored by one who understands the beginning band, makes excellent playing material for this grade level.

Philip Gordon: *A Little Shakespeare Suite*
Grade II 2:45 Theodore Presser

Arranged in *fast, slow, fast* format, the three short pieces of this suite are based on songs used in the original productions of Shakespeare's *Twelfth Night*, *The Merry Wives of Windsor*, and *Much Ado About Nothing*. The teaching approach could go beyond the usual musical preparation, including dramatization of the sections of the plays in which the music occurs. This music would make a fine beginning for the study of Elizabethan music. All the movements are homophonic in texture. Players will be challenged to produce a light, crisp articulation; accidentals in the central movement should promote a keen awareness of enharmonic thinking.

Morton Gould: *Mini Suite*
Grade II 4:30 Chappell

Taken from three contrasting piano pieces, this edition is very tasteful and musically interesting for young band. The construction and texture of the music is simple, yet many passages and sections require delicate and lightly controlled playing. The first movement is in march form, while the second, a waltz, is expressive, requiring a more gentle hand. The final movement, *Bell Carol*, is energetic; marcato style of playing is called for.

Percy Grainger/Glenn Cliffe Bainum:
Australian Up-Country Tune
Grade III 2:00 G. Schirmer

The tune is original, written by Grainger in 1905. The music is warm, rich, and free, possessing a lyrical grace. Constant use of changing meters (2/4, 3/4, 4/4, 2/4) provides challenge. Percussion requirements are minimal: only timpani. This work gives the conductor the opportunity to play Grainger with even young players.

Percy Grainger: *Ye Banks and Ye Braes 'O Bonnie Doon*
Grade III 2:45 G. Schirmer

Only thirty measures long, in 6/8 time, this beautiful and colorful folk tune arrangement is of the highest quality; the melody is a Scottish folk-song of exceptional character. Instrumental technique is not the issue; rather, it is control to avoid harshness. Horns are central to this music, and at least one horn player must sustain (with good pitch) written high g. In the final measures only, first Bb clarinet is written to high a (the space above the fourth leger line), doubling Eb clarinet. However, as this merely doubles the flutes, it could reasonably be reassigned in Bb clarient an octave down; hence this need not be a technical issue for young band. (Elsewhere, clarinet ranges are within Grade III levels.) Percussion requirements are one suspended cymbal. Harmonium or organ is optional.

Martin M. Greene: *Tina Singu*
Grade I 2:30 Pro Art Publications

Syncopation and block scoring dominate this version of an African folk song. Driving opening and final sections of the arrangement are sharply contrasted with a rich, lyrical middle section. This work demands modest technical skill and is an excellent vehicle to use toward blending group phrasing and dynamics.

Edvard Grieg/John Constantine: *Two Lyric Pieces*
Grade III 2:30 Theodore Presser

This is an arrangement of Grieg's "Song of Patriots" (Op. 12, No. 8) and "Norwegian Melody" (Op. 12, No. 6). The tempos are brisk, slurs are rare, and many accent and staccato marks are present. The pieces are an excellent means for training production of sudden dynamic changes and sensitivity to constant changes in scoring. This is fine music arranged with sensitivity and care.

Clare Grundman: *American Folk Rhapsody No. 1*
Grade III 6:15 Boosey & Hawkes

In this first of many folk rhapsodies, Grundman masters the art of writing rich-sounding music for young band, without presenting excessive technical obstacles. Melodies of four American folk songs, "My Little Mohee," "Shantyman's Life," "Sourwood Mountain," and "Sweet Betsy from Pike" are provided with lush countermelodies and appropriate settings. Students will be challenged to play in several styles ranging from lyrical, to light, to legato. This medley is straightforward and is easily attainable by many younger ensembles.

Clare Grundman: *American Folk Rhapsody No. 2*
Grade III 6:30 Boosey & Hawkes

An exquisite medley of three cherished American folk songs, this folk rhapsody is enjoyable to perform and listen to, combining "Billy Boy," "Skip to My Lou," and "Shenandoah" in unique musical settings. "Billy Boy" is given a simple, straightforward statement of the melody, while the melody of "Skip to My Lou" is varied several times in a light-hearted fashion. "Shenandoah" is presented with countermelody and full accompaniment requiring sensitivity and musicianship from the clarinets and the baritones. The popularity of the folk songs contained in this medley make it a favorite of Grundman's *Folk Rhapsodies*.

Clare Grundman: *American Folk Rhapsody No. 3*
Grade III 6:45 Boosey & Hawkes

This third folk rhapsody is an attractive musical scenario, a collection of "Colorado Trail," "Git Along, Little Dogies," "Careless Love," and "Turkey in the Straw." Transitions from song to song are smooth and musical. However, key centers of C, F, G and Bb may provide a very real technical and listening challenge to younger musicians. This is good music with interest and appeal. In the hands of the skillful ensemble, it will become enjoyable playing, and it should be well received.

Clare Grundman: *American Folk Rhapsody No. 4*
Grade III 5:30 Boosey & Hawkes

In this fourth and final rhapsody, the quicker songs, "Little Brown Jug" and "Hey, Betty Martin, Tiptoe, Tiptoe" are more thickly scored than the slower songs, "Down in the Valley" and "Rosie Nell." There are solos for piccolo, flute, oboe, cornet and horn, all well designed. The music is tasteful and enjoyable.

Clare Grundman: *The Blue and the Gray (Civil War Suite)*
Grade III 9:00 Boosey & Hawkes

This suite presents nine songs from the American Civil War era with occasional percussion interludes between the songs. Because they are familiar folk songs that are readily available, their texts can be studied to aid in the understanding of the spirit, style and interpretation. The entire band must have a fluent technique and a good rhythmic vocabulary to perform this music. Although this suite may be difficult for some Grade III bands, it is worthy of rehearsal time. Familiar melodic material will allow the students to stretch their capabilities in technical and interpretive ways.

Clare Grundman: *Burlesque for Band*
Grade III 2:45 Boosey & Hawkes

This rather playful and humorous score uses quick chromatic runs, trills, glissandos, and imaginative percussion writing to bring the music to life. *Burlesque* exposes a light and musically humorous side of Clare Grundman.

Clare Grundman: *A Colonial Legend*
Grade III 5:30 Boosey & Hawkes

Four songs popular during Colonial America ("Chester," "Boston Tea Party," "Yankee Doodle," and "America") are cleverly arranged in this medley. Although difficult technical passages are not evident here, each section must perform with strong playing. Solos from piccolo, bassoon, horn, cornet, baritone, and bells are called for, while a wide variety of percussion instruments, including keyboard mallet, are important. The work is a challenge for a good ensemble.

Clare Grundman: *Fantasy on American Sailing Songs*
Grade III 6:30 Boosey & Hawkes

This collection of folk songs will be very challenging for even the most skilled young bands. A progression of several key shifts and various tempi and meters, including a short section in 12/8, will be the major technical issues. The largest musical challenge will be to make a continuing musical flow through each of the rather short folk tunes. There is aesthetic character here, and both conductor and player must be precise and careful in the execution of these tempo shifts to bring the music to life in a way that does not reveal the seams between tunes.

Clare Grundman: *Hebrides Suite*
Grade III   7:00   Boosey & Hawkes

This suite is an arrangement of airs from M. Kennedy-Fraser's collection, *Songs of the Hebrides*. Grundman's gift for technically modest but musically rich and original writing makes this piece extremely well suited for young musicians. Although written for full band, its delicate flavor may make it more suitable for a smaller grouping of winds and percussion. All the songs have a distinct English flavor. The suite is in four movements: The first, in minor mode, requires crisp, rhythmic, dignified playing; the second presents a simple legato cornet melody over an arpeggiated woodwind accompaniment; the third consists of short motifs playfully passed among instruments; the fourth is march-like, featuring dotted and reverse dotted (so-called ''Scotch snap'') rhythms. Steady tempo and sharp rhythm are the main challenges facing the young band. The stylistic and musical depth make this work an outstanding addition to the young band repertoire.

Clare Grundman: *An Irish Rhapsody*
Grade III   6:00   Boosey & Hawkes

This rhapsody is a fine example of Grundman's gift for writing beautiful countermelodies. Each of the six Irish folk songs is presented in a lush harmonic setting with active inner voices; dissonance and resolution propels the music forward. The resourceful conductor can enhance the musical understanding of this piece by researching the many excellent folk recordings of these songs.

Clare Grundman: *Japanese Rhapsody*
Grade III   5:00   Boosey & Hawkes

This is a collection of three Japanese folk melodies. Two of the songs are lively, animated statements, while the third is slower, very legato, with a contemplative upper woodwind melody. This is an appealing suite, built around pentatonic key centers. It is good concert music, and can well serve as a springboard to the study of Japanese music.

Clare Grundman: *Little Suite for Band*
Grade II   4:30   Boosey & Hawkes

This three-movement (*fast, slow, fast*) suite presents little technical challenge and is ideally suited to elementary or junior high band with lesser skill development. The *Prelude* is fanfare-like with full and brilliant scoring; *Ballad* has a long, lyrical, muted cornet solo (cross-cued in flute and oboe); *Festival* is spirited, with brass melody and woodwind accompaniment.

Clare Grundman: *A Medieval Story*
Grade II   3:15   Boosey & Hawkes

This composition evokes images of ''heraldry'' throughout. All melodic material is based on a three note accented motif presented in the first measure by the entire brass section. Except for a short legato section in the middle of the piece, a high energy-level is maintained throughout. A strong brass section with good range and endurance is required for performance. With its flare for pageantry, this piece can serve a variety of needs, and is certainly worthy of being programmed.

Clare Grundman: *Two American Songs*
Grade II   3:15   Boosey & Hawkes

Blocked scoring throughout makes this two-movement piece one of Grundman's easier folk song settings, for it requires less musical independence from young instrumentalists. The two songs are in direct contrast, both in meter and in style. ''Common Bill'' requires delicate legato playing, while ''Little Brown Jug'' requires light and separated playing. While an experienced band would be able to perform this work with little rehearsal time, there is much to be learned here for a younger, less skilled ensemble.

Clare Grundman: *Two Irish Songs*
Grade III   3:30   Boosey & Hawkes

The Irish folk songs upon which this music is based are ''The Old Woman'' and ''Over There.'' The former is a bright, staccato melody requiring light and technically advanced playing from the entire ensemble; flowing legato lines encourage musically expressive playing in the latter. This work demonstrates the arranger's skills in writing rich harmonies, singing countermelodies, and sound orchestrations.

Clare Grundman: *Two Moods*
Grade II   3:20   Boosey & Hawkes

Though *Two Moods* is one of Grundman's earlier works, it stands today as a staple of young band literature. A sharp contrast between the opening lyric section of this piece and the march-like closing section provides a wealth of teaching material for the young ensemble. With the exception of one muted cornet passage, there is little solo or exposed section playing, allowing for the development of ensemble stability and security. Because the technical demands are modest, rehearsal time can be best spent on phrasing and interpretation. This Grundman ''classic'' is good material for concert or contest.

Clare Grundman: *A Westchester Overture*
Grade III 3:30 Boosey & Hawkes

Full scoring throughout this overture creates a rich and vibrant sound. A recurring three-note chromatic motif provides continuity and a base for melodic development. Lyrical woodwind and cornet melodies dominate, usually accompanied by sharply articulated rhythmic figures in the upper and lower voices. This overture is excellent for concert use since it is both exciting to play, and "listenable."

Donald Haddad: *Mini-Suite No. 1*
Grade II 3:40 Southern Music

There a wealth of teaching possibilities in this short two-movement suite. Both *Pavane*, a slow, mainly homophonic movement, requiring sustained and sensitive playing, and *March*, a movement requiring detached yet resonant playing, are modal in nature with many "ear-stretching" but beautiful harmonies. The success of this suite depends both on stylistic understanding and attention to dynamic and articulation markings. It is a fine piece for the musical development of a young band.

George Frideric Handel/Andrew Balent: *Chaconne with 13 Variations*
Grade III 4:00 Bourne Publishing

The arranger has selected 13 variations from the original 64 contained in Handel's work for keyboard instruments. Despite an unchanging variation length of eight measures, there is a wonderful variety. All players must be able to sustain strong lines for those eight measure phrases. Solo passages are included for oboe and clarinet. This is an excellent vehicle for the study of variation technique, especially if the conductor exposes his students to the original keyboard chaconne in its entirety. Players need a controlled, mature sound without straining.

Howard Hanson: *Variations on an Ancient Hymn*
Grade III 3:00 Carl Fischer

Howard Hanson's music is highly regarded; his compositions for all media leave little doubt of his renowned position in the musical world. For those who savor his romantic *Chorale and Alleluia*, this piece will engender many similar feelings. Frequent meter changes (5/4, 6/4, 4/4) may present early rehearsal problems, which should be overcome with practice. Primary performance concerns will come from the need to sustain long, expressive phrases and sonorities with acceptable tone and pitch. If these demands can be met, a rewarding experience should result.

Robert Hanson: *Four French Songs*
Grade III 6:12 Southern Music

This work is based on four sixteenth-century chansons. The songs are presented in their original modes, and sometimes the cadences are unusual or unexpected. In teaching madrigal style, the creative director may wish to locate vocal recordings of similar songs of the sixteenth century to serve as examples. This style of music is rarely encountered in young band literature. It will familiarize students with a variety of tempi, meters, and modes.

Gerald Hartley: *A Fuguing Tune*
Grade III 2:45 Shawnee Press

Drawing upon the energy and vitality of early American composer William Billings' fuguing tunes, but original in content, Hartley's music is a freely-structured fugue. The opening thematic material is introduced in the clarinets and subsequently tossed among instrument families in a most effective way. The rhythmic structure propels the work forward in a spirited way, while g minor makes the piece technically quite playable.

Ross Hastings: *Dance on Three Legs*
Grade II 2:30 Alfred Publishing

This delightful dance in 5/4 time gives both conductor and players a welcome departure from duple and triple meter band music. The unusual meter, together with the chromatic alterations, will provide a good measure of challenge. The scoring of this music is fresh, calling for four-measure sequences by full band alternating with various instrumental groupings. Percussion writing is not only busy, but appealing.

Brent Heisinger: *Hymn for Band*
Grade III 4:00 Shawnee Press

This beautiful hymn is a challenge to the musicianship and sensitivity of any ensemble. The thematic material is presented in the Dorian mode and is accompanied mainly by tertian harmonies and chords based on open fifths. Much of the thematic material is presented by soloists with little or no accompaniment. Dissonance, a low tessitura, and a slow tempo all characterize this liturgical piece, which is furthermore rich in warmth and musicality.

Brent Heisinger: *Soliloquy for Band*
Grade III 3:35 Shawnee Press

Aptly named, *Soliloquy* consists mainly of solitary instruments presenting melodic ideas, with occasional contrasting tutti sections. With a single modal line as the basic melodic material, this piece winds through homophonic and polyphonic textures, several tonalities, and varied levels of intensity to create an interesting fabric in time. Young virtuoso playing is required from the clarinets, alto saxophone, low woodwinds, and baritone. Playing with a full, sustained sound will present the greatest challenge in this rich composition for band.

Sydney Hodkinson: *A Contemporary Primer for Band*
   (Volumes One and Two)
Grade I-III various durations Theodore Presser

Hodkinson's excellent series of primers (there are three volumes: I-Preliminary Studies, II-Intermediate Studies, III-Advanced Studies, which is itself beyond Grade III) are of both pedagogical and performance value. The basic approach is to teach the student new ideas in a "learn column," and then to apply these ideas to the playing of an actual piece. The text is easy to read, very understandable, and readily performable. What makes this book special is that only contemporary ("avant garde") music is covered. As the preface to Volume I states, "The newer concepts of melody, density, tone-color and notation, with which composers have been dealing for the last half-century, have been largely ignored." It is to this task that the *Contemporary Primer* sets itself, and with considerable success. For six players to full band.

Sydney Hodkinson: *Stone Images*
Grade II 5:00 Merion Music

The stone images of the title are "vast ceremonial ruins" such as Stonehenge, which are "huge, never-changing, yet constantly different." The "static, frozen musical sounds" are Hodkinson's attempt to "evoke these mammoth shapes." The notation is proportional, and the music is aleatoric to some degree. Technical requirements are minimal, thereby giving opportunity to focus on color, texture, and creativity. Instructions to the conductor are detailed, practical, readable, and musical, and a lesson plan of suggested rehearsal techniques is most helpful. After the completion of Volume I of the composer's *Contemporary Primer*, *Stone Images* is *the* work to perform.

Sydney Hodkinson: *Tower*
Grade III 7:00 Merion Music

Tower, the sixth in Hodkinson's series of "megalithic" pieces, in proportional metric notation, is more difficult than *Stone Images*. The moments of new sounds, individual expression, and ensemble tension and release make this more advanced Hodkinson piece well worth the rehearsal time required for performance. One interesting feature of the preface is a re-notation of a couple of measures of proportional metric notation into standard symbolic notation *at two slightly different tempos*. This demonstrates how much simpler certain "complex" rhythms appear when notated proportionally.

Alan Hovhaness: *Suite for Band*
Grade III 10:00 C.F. Peters

Traditions of early religious music are clearly evident in this unusual six-movement suite. Each solemn movement reflects the composer's study of ancient American music, using a wide variety of modes and compositional techniques ranging from chant and organum to fugal development. A strong and musically mature low brass and cornet section are essential for performance, as often they carry an ornamented melody over a drone in several other voices. This musically rich suite could serve as a springboard to the study of early religious music. Studied in part or as a whole, the unusual sonorities found in this suite provide good wind music for younger bands.

Alan Hovhaness: *Tapor No. 1*
Grade II 3:30 C.F. Peters

This beautiful, procession-like music is a true test for brass players, who must play with a large and full sound. The independent, polyphonic parts, require secure players, although there are no real rhythmic problems. The writing is very idiomatic for all instruments, and the rich, sonorous sounds will make this an extremely well-liked and versatile piece.

Anthony Iannaccone: *Plymouth Trilogy*
Grade III 8:00 Ludwig Music Publishing

Plymouth Trilogy is written by a composer who understands the band, and younger players in particular. The opening, marchlike 6/8 movement (which contains flute solos) presents melodic fragments upon which the other movements are based; the second movement (which contains a solo cornet line) is extremely slow (quarter note equals 40) and requires the players to play with sensitivity and restraint; the third movement is a spirited, syncopated rag. Although ranges are not excessive, technical skill is mandatory: Fluent, intelligent technique, especially in the finale, is needed to bring this music to life.

Charles Ives/Jonathan Elkus: *Old Home Days*
Grade III 8:30 Peer International

This five-movement suite reflects Ives' lifelong love of familiar tunes and homegrown music-making. All the movements are masterfully scored utilizing the best of the full ensemble, yet retaining independent lines. The idiomatic flavor, charm, and humor of Ives' music has been skillfully retained in this arrangement. The teaching material is very challenging, but well worth the effort. A superbly published 10½ by 14 inch full score is an integral aspect of this first-rate repertoire for younger players.

Charles Ives/Jonathan Elkus: *A Son of a Gambolier*
Grade III 6:00 Peer International

With all the touches and style of an Irish dance tune, this arrangement skillfully captures the Ives irregular, off-center phrase structure, as well as his nonchalance and touch of the raucous. Basic 6/8 rhythms in the music can easily be grasped by younger players. Syncopation, cross-accenting, and nuance will provide the greatest challenges for conductor and player alike. The conductor has the choice of following Ives in spirit by adding (optional) corps of players on combs, slide whistles, and "kazoo chorus – flutes, fiddles and flageolets."

Gordon Jacob: *Suite in B Flat*
Grade III 8:00 R. Smith & Co.

The band compositions and orchestrations of Gordon Jacob personify the aesthetic musical direction that wind bands have taken the past three decades. The *Suite in B Flat* reveals the Jacob craftsmanship, clarity, and sonorous wind orchestration. The first movement, *March* (quarter note equals 108), is quite stately, melodic, and harmonically warm. The second movement, *Solemn Music* (quarter note equals 56), is more formal, with a reverent character, and with an important technical consideration for younger players—a key signature of (concert) five flats, and long sustained phrases, which will keep them attentive and musicianly. The *Finale* (quarter note equals 132) combines elements of lightness and smooth, legato playing into a satisfying conclusion.

Louis E. Jadin/William Schaeffer: *Symphonie for Band*
Grade III 3:00 Shawnee Press

Written in 1794, this symphony is in one movement, and in form is more closely aligned to an overture. The key center is F major, with occasional modulations to closely related keys. The major performance problem will be achieving the necessary light and crisp style. Players and conductor will have to discipline themselves to avoid excessive levels of sound. This music, here rescored for modern symphonic band, is from a very important historical period in the evolution of wind band music, and most certainly should be included in the performance repertoire of all bands, regardless of age level or performing grade.

Robert Jager: *Japanese Prints*
Grade II 6:30 Edward B. Marks Music

Facets of Japanese life are depicted in three predominantly pentatonic movements: *Kiyomizu* depicts a powerful and impressive temple shrine through fiery tempos and heavily accented brass. *Yumi Kato* describes a peaceful and gentle Japanese girl who performs tea ceremonies. Many percussion instruments are employed to give a Japanese flavor to the proceedings. There are frequent meter changes (2/4, 3/4, 4/4) in the first two movements. *Kodama* depicts the Japanese bullet trains. The steady, rhythmic accompaniment figures evoke images of the trains, and build to an exciting and dynamic conclusion.

Douglas K. Jones: *Interlochen Variations*
Grade III 6:00 TRN Music

This is a wonderful piece for the very mature young band. The composer's sense of theme and variation structure and effective orchestration is well-documented here. A strong horn section is necessary, and the demands on all sections are heavy. The percussion writing is imaginative and players will be quite active throughout. The music unwinds itself from variation to variation, culminating in a broad and exciting ending.

Dmitri Kabalevsky/Seikman & Oliver: *Six Episodes*
Grade I 4:15 MCA Music

This suite of six rather short movements is characteristic of more advanced music of its genre and contains a variety of stylistic and contrasting musical constructs. Its orchestration and technical demands are extremely well-conceived for the very early instrumentalists. This is music which is attainable by the beginning band in its early stages of ensemble playing.

Dmitri Kabalevsky/Seikman & Oliver: *Suite in Minor Mode*
Grade II 4:00 MCA Music

The three piano pieces upon which this suite is based are all in minor mode and follow a *fast, slow, fast* scheme. This music has a freshness and simplicity, making it an attractive offering. The prevailing minor tonalities help make this ideal teaching material for young bands.

John Kinyon: *English Hunting Song*
Grade I 2:00 Alfred Publishing

This short piece is shaped in a simple *ABA* form. The harmonic setting is major, with B-flat and E-flat as key centers. The score has a very *cantabile* nature and youngsters should find its content very accessible and musically enjoyable. This ia good piece for the very early band.

John Kinyon: *Festivity*
Grade II 3:20 Alfred Publishing

This is a festive piece for younger players complete with syncopated dance rhythms (the latin *clave* pattern predominates), and a sparkling ostinato. The form is *ABA*, the *A* a spirited dance *con fuoco* in Dorian mode, the *B* more free and lush, in major mode. Scoring is safe, with instrumentation well-suited to younger ensembles, with ample cross-cuing throughout.

John Kinyon: *A Londonderry Air*
Grade I 3:05 Alfred Publishing

Kinyon's rendition of this old Irish folk song features the clarinet section. They begin with unison melody, accompanied by beautiful countermelodies in flutes. The song builds to an emotional climax using the sonorous full band sound and ends again with the clarinet melody. This piece provides great opportunity for development of musically sensitive playing, both for individuals and the ensemble as a whole.

John Kinyon: *Pageantry for Band*
Grade I 2:20 Alfred Publishing

Beginning with a fanfare, this marchlike music unfolds in a straightforward manner, making it suitable for the very early full ensemble experience. The scoring is safe, requiring little if any musical independence from any instrumental group, and is thus ideal for bands lacking complete instrumentation. Ranges and technical requirements are likewise within the grasp of first-year instrumentalists.

John Kinyon: *Set of Early English Airs*
Grade II 4:00 Boosey & Hawkes

John Adson, Henry Purcell, and Anthony Holborne occupy important positions in the Baroque pantheon. In the skillful pen of John Kinyon, their superbly crafted short airs, pavanes, and dances, become vital musical material for young players. The ample cross-cuing allows the conductor to accommodate smaller and incomplete bands.

Raymond L. Kirby: *San Pei Folk Song March*
Grade II 4:00 TRN Music

The folk tune from the North Shensi Province of China upon which this work is based may remind some of Sullivan's marchlike tunes from *The Mikado*. Such is the simple and "catchy" nature of the joyous pentatonic tunes of this work. An inventive orchestration creates interesting interplay among sections without unduly exposing any particular instrumental choir. The chief performance requirement is retaining a spirited, accented, detached style, and a reasonably upbeat tempo; otherwise, the work could sound plodding and overly heavy. Parts for castanets, Chinese cymbal, clappers, and gong add to an authentic flavor. Your students will enjoy the change of pace, and your audience will surely be intrigued by this charming and decidedly different concert fare.

Pierre LaPlante: *Overture on a Minstrel Tune*
Grade III 3:15 Bourne Publishing

A surprising amount of polyphony is to be found in this minstrel tune arrangement. The polyphonic texture and the very active parts for all the players make this "foot-tapping" music worthy of study. This is short and delightful music.

William Latham: *Court Festival*
Grade III 4:30 Summy-Birchard

Four short movements constitute this suite based upon the form and style of sixteenth and seventeenth century instrumental dances. This impressive work is masterfully scored for band; the woodwinds are treated very idiomatically and therefore must play with fluent technique; the percussion writing is delicate and graceful. The last movement is based upon an actual Renaissance tune, a *Bransle* from Arbeau's *Orchesographie* (1589), and is scored in the first sixteen measures for solo piccolo, bassoons, and tabor drum. This is a most stylistically demanding and musically sensitive piece of wind music.

William Latham: *Dodecaphonic Set*
Grade III 4:20 C.L. Barnhouse

The subtitle of this work is *Five Twelve-Tone Pieces for Band*; the music is rich in melodic thought and harmonic color. The writing is not disjoint and pointillistic, but rather motivic and melodic, sometimes almost Bartokian, and hence more easily accessible to players and audience than the usually more austere dodecaphonic constructs of, for example, a Schoenberg. This is a contemporary work that will appeal to the mature young band and the serious-minded conductor.

Jean Baptiste Lully/Livingston & Forsblad: *Two Intermezzi*
Grade II 3:15 Theodore Presser

This rather short, two-movement piece from the *comedies-ballets* of Lully provides a fine opportunity to explore simple Baroque dance music. This music, co-arranged by Wayne Livingston and Leland Forsblad, is well within the skills of young players. Independent musicianship is not the issue in this piece; musical intricacy and style is.

Bob Margolis (after Claude Gervaise): *Fanfare Ode & Festival*
Grade II 4:00 Manhattan Beach Music

This wonderful three-movement setting of early dances is based upon music published by Pierre Attaignant in a six-volume collection entitled *Danceries* (1555). The music is fresh, cast with rich textures and expansive sonorities. The score is a masterful presentation in orchestration, and it is music well-suited to the needs of young players. The preface and opening remarks also provide a wealth of information. This is a "must" piece in the young band/wind ensemble repertoire.

Bob Margolis: *Prelude and March*
Grade I   2:15   Manhattan Beach Music

This is an attractive piece for young band in that the writing is clear, fresh, and transparent. The *Prelude*, which has the sound of a dirge, opens quietly for flutes; added to this are sensitive accompanying lines, and soft percussion sounds. The g minor *March* is a rather atypical setting, in that it is mischievous, quite disjunct, yet exciting. It employs finger snaps, and interesting percussion sounds. The writing here is creative and well-suited to the needs of Grade I performance skills.

David Maslanka: *Rollo Takes A Walk*
Grade III   2:22   Kjos Music

From the gifted composer of *A Child's Garden of Dreams* comes this less intense but musically clever offering. Rollo is a fictional character created by Charles Ives and is used to illustrate "ultra-conservative musical tastes." The musical fabric here is reminiscent of Ives' familiar explorations of town bands. It is purposely out-of-tune or microtonal. The music evokes an an earlier, more innocent era in America's history. The scoring for winds is exceptional, with optional parts for Eb clarinet, contra-bassoon, and Bb contrabass clarinet. Three percussion parts call for as many as 15 various percussion instruments. Complete with several measures of kazoo and short vocal parts, the music is both serious and challenging.

W. Francis McBeth: *Battaglia*
Grade III   5:30   Southern Music

There is emotional content in this single-movement work for junior high band. Beginning with an *Allegro Maestoso* brass statement, the music unfolds into an *ABA Coda* design. The *B* section is rather slow (quarter note equals 58) and more dramatic than the other sections. Here, the ensemble must play with maturity and patience, allowing the music to return to the more powerful *A* section. This music is composed by one who knows the band well; the design is for youngsters, and it is music deserving of performance and study.

W. Francis McBeth: *Cavata*
Grade II   5:00   Southern Music

This composition is representative of a genre of pieces for junior high band in that its scoring and instrumentation demands are solid and safe. Its *ABA* form, its triadic harmonies, unison melodies, and propelling percussion writing will give the young ensemble an exciting sound. There are sensitive moments in the slower middle section, and the piece comprises a number of musical constructs important in developing musicianship.

W. Francis McBeth: *Chant and Jubilo*
Grade III   7:00   Southern Music

This piece in two contrasting sections has for years been a program favorite of many junior high school band conductors. The opening chant contains many elements of Gregorian chant and early church *organum*. The serene chanting moves into a rather festive, *jubilante* section with trumpet calls and a driving rhythmic percussion ostinato. The piece culminates in a beautifully scored chordal section. There are no major technical pitfalls in this music, although the ensemble must be mature in sound, with a fluent and controlled technique.

Frank McCarty: *Exitus for Band*
Grade III   7:00   Joseph Boonin

Exitus is an aleatoric "sound piece" which utilizes vocal sounds processed through wind instruments. The piece is written in graphic and symbolic notation that does not use the traditional musical staff. A very good and clear set of instructions for interpreting the symbols is included in the score. The piece is unique in that the sounds and various freedoms given to the players open new musical concepts. Players can benefit greatly from the experiences offered here; they will build skills necessary for dealing with further contemporary music.

Anne McGinty: *Encomium*
Grade II   4:30   Hal Leonard Publishing

This overture-like piece, with its *fast, slow, fast* design, is music that interweaves contrasting *heroic* and *reflective* moods into a modified sonata form. The basic harmonic scheme is F Major alternating with C Major, Bb Major, and D Major. However, all necessary accidentals have been written in, thereby decreasing the likelihood of persistent key problems. Except for rapid tongued passages of some sixteenth notes in the winds, and frequent modulations, the piece is easily playable by Grade II bands. It is music which should be learned with minimal rehearsal time.

Theldon Meyers: *From An 18th Century Album*
Grade II   4:30   TRN Music

Three rather obscure 18th-century composers provide the original material found in this suite. Neefe, Hiller, and Reichardt's music may not be as familiar as their 18th century contemporaries, but their musical craft is representative of the time. Delicacy and lightness of articulation and style are the major teaching problems. No special instrumentation is required, and ranges and technical concerns are attainable by younger musicians. Not surprisingly, percussion writing is modest; however, percussion is important and must, of course, be subtle and refined.

Donal Michalsky: *Little Symphony for Band*
Grade III   12:00   Donal Michalsky, manuscript

Written in 1959 as a commission from the La Canada (California) Junior High School, this piece is a major work for young band. In structuring the tonal base, Michalsky utilized the pitches A, B, E, Eb, A, D, A, C, A, A, D, A, all chosen from the conductor's name, Larry Bellis, and the school's name, La Canada. The four-movement work is an exhilarating combination of sounds and textures. The rhythmic constructs are relatively simple, although a variety of meter signatures make the rhythmic flow interesting to perform. Conductors looking for outstanding structure, uniqueness of tonality, and aesthetic direction will enjoy this music.

Eugene Mitchell: *Listen to the Lambs*
Grade II   2:00   Belwin-Mills Publishing

This setting of a spiritual presents a sensitive chorale-style statement and a faster, rock-style development of the same theme, all very conventional in approach and easy for young players to grasp. Though familiar compositional devices are present here, the piece may be used to teach division of the beat, particularly as it relates to syncopation. In addition, articulations and musical style are important teaching concepts in this music.

Mozart/John Cacavas: *Allegro and Dance*
Grade I   3:00   Theodore Presser

These two Mozart works are skillfully arranged, with each retaining its characteristic lightness and clarity of line. The major teaching problem is musical style. Each player will need to perform with proper idiomatic thought in order to retain the transparent quality of this music. Ensemble writing for full band generally predominates. However, because of ample doubling, the conductor may wish to choose a smaller wind ensemble combination to better achieve the appropriate musical style.

Mozart/Philip Gordon: *Minuet and Country Dance*
Grade I   3:30   Theodore Presser

The tuneful *Minuet* has been well edited as to articulations; the sprightly and somewhat martial *Country Dance*, likewise, making this edition good teaching material. Ranges and technical problems are very well thought through, giving youngsters the luxury of focusing their practice on style.

Vaclav Nelhybel: *Chorale*
Grade III   4:30   Franco Colombo Publications

This is a wonderful piece that only the most mature and skillful young band should perform. It is based upon a medieval Bohemian chant whose words are a desperate plea to St. Wenceslaus, the first king of Bohemia, not to forsake his people nor let them perish. The aesthetic character of the music is found in the growth of instrumental groupings playing sustained crescendos and diminuendos against the ancient chant, thereby musically representing the pleas of the people. Control and intonation are the watchwords in performance. The music is rich in sound and will enhance the musical growth of any ensemble.

Vaclav Nelhybel: *Fantasia* .
Grade III   5:00   J. Christopher Music

This original composition in three sections is based upon J.S. Bach's Prelude No. 1 from the *Well-Tempered Clavier*. The contrapuntal aspects of this music will provide the biggest performance problem for the players. All players, including percussionists, will have to perform with care, sensitivity, maturity and patience. The trumpet part calls for extended range and intelligent technique, while other parts are well within the capabilities of young players. This exciting piece is worth the needed rehearsal time for concert.

Vaclav Nelhybel: *Festivo*
Grade III   6:00   Franco Colombo Publications

A longtime favorite of many junior high school band conductors, *Festivo* is a high-energy-level piece. Nelhybel himself states that the piece is a constant confrontation of woodwinds and brasses, ''like two antagonists in a dramatic scene.'' The percussion parts require a rapid stick technique, yet are playable by even young percussionists. For conductors searching for an overture-type piece with forward momentum, quick tempi, and high energy, this piece will work.

Vaclav Nelhybel: *Suite Concertante*
Grade III   10:00   Franco Colombo Publications

Each group of wind instruments throughout the band is used as the *concertino* group in this five-movement work. As in much of Nelhybel's band music, strong players are required throughout, especially in percussion, where the parts are musical and imaginative. Since the music is built upon the modes, players are given a healthy departure from band music too often written in major tonalities only.

Vaclav Nelhybel: *Suite from Bohemia*
Grade II   8:00   Canyon Press

A composition in four movements, this work reflects differing aspects of Bohemian folk music. Here we see Nelhybel's dramatic expression of embodied Bohemian feeling come to reality for the young wind band. Frequent use of aeolian, mixolydian, and dorian modes with rich harmonies form the sensitivity of the music. Skillful percussion, mature clarinets and brasses form the necessary instrumentation requirements.

Sammy Nestico: *All Through the Night*
Grade II   3:10   Kendor Music

This arrangement of the well-known song gives instrumentalists an opportunity to play expressively. Emphasizing harmonic richness, legato style, and contour of line, the piece begs for a warm and free interpretation. Good flexibility is required from the flutes and trumpets. However, the requirements placed upon the other instrumentalists are not excessive, and the music should be easily assimilated.

LeRoy Osmon: *Hebrew Folk Song Suite*
Grade II   3:30   TRN Music

Jewish folk and dance music form the basis of this attractive three-movement suite. The tonality of this music is minor, as is characteristic of much Jewish folk music. The melodies are good, tuneful, rhythmically active, and fun to play. The music is scored solidly for winds with an ample sampling of percussion instruments such as finger cymbals and tambourine. This music makes attractive listening, and should provide young players with an enjoyable experience.

Eric Osterling: *Symphonic Chorale*
Grade III   3:00   Chappell

This sensitive, lyrical chorale setting emphasizes linear, expressive playing. A controlled tone quality and lyrical expressiveness are necessary for a gratifying interpretation. The piece depends heavily upon woodwinds, trombones, and baritones for much of the thematic material. Used in rehearsal as a piece for teaching lyrical and sensitive playing, or as a work for concert, it is by all measures musical.

Russell Peck: *Star Machine*
Grade III   3:20   Edward B. Marks Music

With the abundance of "contemporary sound pieces" for advanced wind ensemble/wind bands today, it is crucial for younger musicians to receive an introduction to these concepts. This piece represents a wonderful start towards that aim in that it gives the musicians many of the aural and visual skills necessary for performing more advanced scores, but does not make any significant musical (that is, "ear-stretching") demands upon the players. A carefully written set of new notational symbols is provided for the conductor in the score. The sounds include the use of bowed cymbals and gong; wind sounds; key clatter; and the "highest possible note" concept. The score (in standard five-line-staff symbolic notation, not in proportional or graphic notation) is written in 6/8 and sounds much like a march. This is nevertheless serious music, well-designed for young musicians.

James Ployhar: *A Hundred Pipers*
Grade I   1:45   Carl Fischer

This arrangement is based upon a Scottish melody of L. Lairne. The martial spirit is captured by a crisp snare drum parade cadence and lightly articulated woodwind melodies. Young musicians must play with fluent technique because a fairly rapid tempo must be achieved to bring this piece to life. In addition to its concert programming appeal, the piece is excellent 6/8 teaching material. This is a wonderful piece for the very young.

James Ployhar: *A New Wrinkle on Twinkle*
Grade I   3:00   Belwin-Mills Publishing

This splendid theme and variations is not only useful concert fare, but is educationally invaluable as well. Beginning with a statement of the tune, there follows a waltz (3/4), "swing" (4/4), and concert march (6/8). Pedagogical constructs are predominant over musical ones in this full tutti scoring, making this piece very suitable for the teaching of rhythmic reading skills for beginners, and as "safe" concert fare.

William Rhoads: *Three Russian Cameos*
Grade III 8:00 TRN Music

This three-movement suite features settings of music of Glinka, Maykapar, and Kabalevsky. The first movement is a fast Cossack dance; there is some modest counterpoint present and interesting rhythmic activity for all. The second movement in g minor is slow and sustained: It presents some possibilities for emotionalism. The third movement is the most challenging technically, requiring facile scale patterns in the woodwinds and powerful accents in the brass. The percussion writing (for timpani, snare drum, cymbals, gong, tambourine, and bells) is active and interesting throughout. The ranges and technical concerns of wind instruments are well-suited to younger players.

Willis Schaefer: *Reflections on a Boyhood Summer*
Grade II 5:30 Willis Schaefer, manuscript

This elementary band work would be an outstanding addition to any program. It depicts, in three movements, the school-related memories of the composer. The first movement, *Professional Graduation Processional*, stately and rich, with full scoring, is a fanfare requiring a strong trumpet section. *The Lazy Daze of August* is a legato movement with a clarinet section melody. The *Sort of Square Dance* is a hoe-down with mouthpiece pops from the brass. This spirited movement must be performed with energy. Unusual in this suite is the level of sophistication of the harmonic thought. Presenting a wealth of teaching material in an unusual setting, this work is a unique and exciting piece for young band.

Peter Schmalz: *McFarland Overture*
Grade III 6:00 Peter Schmalz, manuscript

A noble sounding and dignified fanfare begins this overture. Weaving through a *fast, slow, fast* framework, the piece reveals melodic brilliance and rhythmic energy. Technical problems are within the grasp of younger players; nevertheless, mature section playing from trumpets, solo horn and solo oboe are required. The latter two are crucial since cross-cuing or doubling is not provided in the score. Rhythmically clear playing is necessary to reveal the cross accents of the score.

Peter Schmalz: *The Mermaid's Comb*
Grade III 5:30 Peter Schmalz, manuscript

Based on a story by Hartley Neita, the music is based on modal tonal base and a free treatment of several motifs. *Allegro* tempos dominate, yielding a spirited framework for the players, whose technical skill will be an issue. The music calls for some aleatoric effects, strong sectional playing throughout, and skillful solo playing in the flute and xylophone. Careful attention to detail, and for the conductor, careful blending of motifs and tempos, will make this composition well worth performance time.

Alexander Schreiner/Earl Slocum: *Lyric Interlude*
Grade III 5:00 TRN Music

Steeped in the Romantic style, this music is slow and reflective, requiring sustained linear playing. Set in *ABA* form, the outer sections (quarter note equals 44) are in Db Major, while the middle section (about twice the tempo) is in A minor. Harmonically, this music is interesting as it shifts through many tonal centers. This is a good piece for exploring the slow, rubato, Romantic style, but because of the keys, tempi, and long sustained lines, a more mature band is required for concert performance.

William Schuman: *The Band Song*
Grade II 3:30 Theodore Presser

This 3/4-time Tyrolian-flavored composition is most familiar to students under the title, "The Instruments," and as such it is often used in general music classes. The various instrumental sections are successively highlighted, each being given characteristic versions of the tune: For example, the trumpets have a little double-tonguing, and the flutes have an arpeggiated version. The themes and the variations occur simultaneously for a delightful melody plus countermelody polyphonic effect. This is a clever work that will be enjoyed by all.

Bedrich Smetana/Philip Gordon: *Rustic Dance*
Grade II 3:00 Theodore Presser

Contrasts fill this piece; players must perform powerfully, gently, loudly, softly, crisply, and smoothly. Tempos range from fast to very fast. It is because of these considerations that technique must be fluent, and interpretation, intelligent. There is thus much to glean from this Czechoslovakian folk dance.

Hale Smith: *Trinal Dance*
Grade II 3:20 MCA Music

A lyrical eight-measure melody in natural minor supplies much of the melodic material for this unusual dance. The rhythmic pulse is provided by a single tambourine; otherwise, the piece is filled with stretched-out legato melodies. Occasionally a four-measure articulated melody recurs among the legato melodies, providing contrast and a clearer sense of rhythmic structure. Younger musicians should enjoy this piece if the rhythmic sensitivity can be assimilated into a "natural" spirit.

Jared Spears: *Meditation and Festiva*
Grade III 4:20 C.L. Barnhouse

A chant-like melody with percussion accompaniment begins this fine concert piece for young band. Gradually, the melodic speed of the *Meditation* increases and the scoring thickens, eventually bursting into a fast, articulated section with heavily syncopated melodies. Frequent accidentals may pose problems. Attention to articulation and dynamic markings can help to insure an inspiring performance of this exciting, well-written piece.

Jared Spears: *Scenario*
Grade III 6:00 Southern Music

This attractive piece places much importance on the percussion section, requiring timpani, snare drum, bass drum, triangle, cymbal (suspended), gong, tom-toms, bells, chimes, and xylophone. A modest timpani solo tying the *B* section of the ternary form to the repeat of the *A* section is the important solo in the piece. There is a welcome emphasis on the inner voices in the band (saxophones, horns, and baritones). The fast sections are quite energetic, with a great deal of syncopation. Dynamic control is especially important, as the composer often calls for sudden contrasts.

Halsey Stevens/William Schaefer: *Ukrainian Folk Songs*
Grade III 11:30 TRN Music

This collection is comprised of eleven movements, each not more than a minute in length. The score is a result of a collaboration of the distinguished composer Halsey Stevens and the skillful arranger William Schaefer. The setting is cleverly done and is indeed fresh, transparent and uncluttered by musical trivia. The score needs to be analyzed for its rhythmic and technical demands; each movement is unique in character. Three or four movements are a bit difficult for Grade III. However, the overall appeal and the attractive musicianship should challenge the best of the younger bands to undertake much, if not all, of the score.

Thomas Stone: *Distant City*
Grade III 3:30 Thomas Stone, manuscript

The conductor of an advanced junior high school band looking for an unusual and challenging work would profit from this manuscript piece. *Distant City* is rhythmically straightforward, lyrical, tonal, and presents a clear-cut *ABA* form, but its polyphonic texture and repeated use of short overlapping motifs makes it unusual band music. Low reeds are essential for producing the wonderfully rich sonorities found in the score, and a solid oboist and trumpeter are necessary. Percussion writing is sparse, and sensitive.

Thomas Stone: *Music for a Sunny Day*
Grade III 3:00 Thomas Stone, manuscript

Set in *ABA* form at a slow tempo, this piece begins pensively with flowing contrapuntal motifs, then builds to an accented and powerful climax, and subsides to a return of the original material. Students will find it enriching to deal with the counterpoint and dramatic intensity found here. Percussion parts are included for timpani, snare and bass drums, tom-toms, bells and suspended cymbal. No horn parts are included; at the discretion of the conductor, it would be possible for horn players to transpose the second alto saxophone part.

Hugh Stuart: *Somerset Sketches*
Grade III 6:45 Boston Music

This delightful three-movement suite (*fast, slow, fast*) is a solid addition to young band literature. Each movement has a folk song flavor, although all of the melodic material found here is original. The first and third movements of this piece provide an opportunity for young instrumentalists to play in "cut time" (2/2). The second movement, *Lullaby*, requires young virtuoso playing from the horns, as legato melodies in their middle and upper register prevail. Sustained legato playing is needed from the band, affording the youngsters a chance to play with musical sensitivity. This work, in the tradition of a folk song suite, is exceptional for young bands.

Hugh Stuart: *Three Ayres from Gloucester*
Grade II 4:30 Shawnee Press

This suite, in the style of early English folk songs, is set in three short movements, each in a different spirit. The first is in *alla breve*, which creates a light-hearted, spirited mood and includes solos for clarinet and cornet. The second is an *andante*, which includes very important (and high) lines for horn, cued into saxophones. The major theme is a gracious melody set over a wonderfully rich low brass and woodwind accompaniment. There is ample opportunity to teach *cantabile* style. The third movement is an allegro-6/8 in the lilting style of the English folk tradition. The entire suite is engagingly written and most gratifying to study, perform, and hear.

Tielman Susato/Bob Margolis: *The Battle Pavane*
Grade II 3:00 Manhattan Beach Music

This arrangement of one of Susato's 16th-century pavanes has retained its characteristic charm and flavor. The main focus of this score is to build the rather calm opening into a triumphant and very broad climax. Because of the rather delicate character of this music, conductors will have to exercise "light-handed" interpretive judgment. An excellent set of program notes is included in the score, making this piece meaningful in a number of ways for younger musicians.

William Svarda: *Dissonants for Band*
Grade III   5:30   Studio P/R

This piece presents some contemporary compositional practices in both harmonic fabric and the use of meters. Much of this music is based upon an ostinato; both 5/4 and 3/2 should enlarge students' metric vocabulary. Sufficient musical energy and excitement is brought about by careful use of tension, release, rhythmic invention, and the subtle use of surprise. The percussion writing for bells, tom-toms, cymbal (suspended), cymbals, snare drum, triangle, bass drum, and timpani is challenging and interesting. Ensemble strength is required from all sections.

John Tatgenhorst: *Canterbury Suite*
Grade III   4:51   C.L. Barnhouse

This single-movement work is in three well-defined sections, resulting in a clear, concise and satisfying form. Full tutti scoring is emphasized. The piece begins and ends with a broad *maestoso*, while the middle provides a more melodic and lyrical contrast. There are no major problems with musical technique in this music, so its rather safe scoring and easily-grasped musical fabric should make it come to reality quickly in rehearsals.

John Tatgenhorst: *Tanglewood*
Grade III   4:20   C.L. Barnhouse

This harmonically rich overture is in a theme-and-variations form. Variation techniques used included retrograde, rhythmic augmentation, addition of parallel thirds to the theme, and various combinations of the above. The theme is modal, providing opportunity for the players to become familiar with Dorian sounds. There are many contrasts ranging from sharp accents to flowing legato melodies, all of which will be useful stylistic teaching tools. This overture is an excellent concert and learning piece.

Piotr Tchaikovsky/Bob Margolis: *Tchaikovsky Album*
Grade III   3:20   Manhattan Beach Music

The three dances of this "album" are taken from Tchaikovsky's *Album for the Young*, Op. 39, for piano. The first song, *Morning Prayer*, is very legato and warm; the second, *March of the Wooden Soldiers*, is march-like yet light; the final *Waltz* is a fitting conclusion to the piece. The technical demands of this music are well-suited to Grade II performance level. However, to accomplish a true reading of the score, young players will be challenged with the various styles present here. Dynamic contrast, execution of articulation, and change of style will require solid effort.

Fred Thayer: *Illumination*
Grade III   5:00   E.C. Schirmer Music

This music was commissioned by a junior high school band, and it is a wonderful addition to a growing repertoire of contemporary literature. The tonal framework is based upon the tone row, with the piece growing clearer tonally as it progresses to its end. Exploration in various sounds are a large part of this score; they include blowing air through instruments, dipping cymbals in water, and the musical use of frying pans. The percussion writing is very imaginative in all aspects, and wind players must demonstrate musical intelligence. A piece for the most mature young band.

Fisher Tull: *Antiphon*
Grade III   3:30   Boosey & Hawkes

The term *antiphony* suggests a responsive alternation between two groups. An opening flourish is followed by contrasting light legato playing. In constructing this piece, Mr. Tull has structured isolated woodwind and brass timbres that enhance the antiphonal character of this work. The piece displays a wonderful sense of scoring, variety, and thematic display, with both wind and percussion writing being imaginative. Careful rehearsal time will make performance a delight.

Clark Tyler: *Simple Gifts*
Grade I   2:30   Alfred Publishing

This setting of the famous Shaker melody is scored rather effectively for the youngest of bands. The melody is presented with a variety of accompaniments, textures, and emotional intents, ranging from simple and gentle to a more poignant and powerful display. The technical demands should not be difficult; the major efforts can be spent on the development of expressive legato playing.

Thomas Tyra: *Modal March, Pentatonic Polka,*
Polytonal Parade, Quartal Caper, Wholey Hymn
Grade I   1:00-2:00 each   C.L. Barnhouse

This excellent learning package has been designed by Thomas Tyra and the editors at Barnhouse to familiarize young bands with some of the important compositional techniques of the 20th century. These pieces, each published separately, are good for concert performance, but their real value lies in the fine ideas for teaching that are included with the scores. An analysis of each piece with ideas for presenting the specific technique(s) highlighted in the piece, a list of listening examples taken from the standard repertoire (mostly piano or orchestra), and ideas for involving students in composition exercises all add greatly to the value of each set. The titles refer to musical construction based on, variously, modal, pentatonic, or whole-tone scales, and polytonal, or quartal harmony. Taken together, or individually, these pieces are a fine resource for the conductor who follows a comprehensive approach to teaching musical concepts.

Thomas Tyra: *Two Gaelic Folk Songs*
Grade III 5:30 C.L. Barnhouse

"Molly Malone" and "The Wearing of the Green" are the two Irish folk songs receiving sensitive settings for band: Melody receives the emphasis in the first; technical possibilities are emphasized in the second. The key of Db Major used in "Molly Malone" is a relief from the more common keys of music of this difficulty. It begins with a statement of the tune for solo horn (cued into both trumpet and saxophone) and builds through repetition and embellishment to a climax in Ab Major, ending softly and precipitously in the same key. The second song presents technical challenges to upper woodwinds and trumpets, both in range and rapid passagework. Considerable time will be required to achieve lightness and accuracy in this section. Thomas Tyra's setting of these popular folk songs is imaginative, full of contrast and surprise.

Ralph Vaughan Williams: *Flourish for Wind Band*
Grade III 1:30 Oxford University Press

It is rare that a composer of this stature and skill writes an easy work for band. Vaughan Williams' *Flourish* works best in a festive occasion, or simply as a concert opener, as it has the character of a fanfare, with a legato middle section. There is a high "a" in solo cornet; and some use of tenor clef in trombone. Otherwise, this music is most playable.

Ralph Vaughan Williams: *Sea Songs*
Grade III 3:20 Boosey & Hawkes

Vaughan Williams' weaving of three sailing songs has produced a piece idiomatic for its time, rich in sonority, and brilliant in its scoring. Concert keys of Ab, Eb, and Db provide a very real technical challenge. This is music from a particularly important period in the development of band repertoire. It offers not only musical depth, but also the study of that genre of literature. Like other British folk songs adapted for band, this piece can be programmed effectively by having a soloist sing the original tunes, which are themselves available in a number of fine editions in a variety of voice ranges.

Ralph Vaughan Williams/Walter Beeler: *Rhosymedre*
Grade III 4:00 Galaxy (see E.C. Schirmer)

In 1920 Vaughan Williams composed three preludes for organ based on Welsh hymn tunes. Of these, *Rhosymedre* has enjoyed the greatest popularity. The piece itself is quite simple, built largely upon scale tones in F Major. The lines are *cantabile* over an obbligato in the bassoon (cross-cued into baritone). The clarinets carry the melody often, but there is adequate melodic depth in the other parts, save of course the low reeds and basses. The playing ranges are not extensive for advancing players, although the first cornet is extended at the climax to high Bb. The nature of the piece keeps percussion writing minimal, and only timpani and chimes are required. This is music of quality, skillfully arranged for band.

Giuseppi Verdi/Ross Hastings: *Emissary Fanfare*
Grade III 2:20 Bourne Publishing

Verdi's simple, triadic fanfare is rich in pomp and bombast. Solo trumpet builds to a sustained "high c," so this piece should not be undertaken unless the right player is available. The musical thought is simple, and the effect upon an audience will be stirring, making this piece useful as a concert opener. Fluent winds and agile brass are musts.

William Walton/Bram Wiggins: *Miniatures for Wind Band*
Grade III 14:00 Oxford University Press

This ten-movement work of contrasting *slow, fast, slow*, etc., is based upon Walton's orchestral piece, *Music for Children*. Each of the ten pieces is thematically and tonally independent; consequently, any number of them could be presented in a program. General playing requirements are significant from each section, with a requirement of fluent, intelligent playing in both woodwinds and brasses. The high quality of Walton's composing is heard in this significant arrangement for band.

Norman Ward: *Suite for Young People*
Grade I 3:40 Belwin-Mills Publishing

This brief four-movement work depicts, in a musical sense, the day in the life of a young child. The music is skillfully scored and the piece affords even the youngest of instrumentalists the opportunity and challenge to play with sensitivity. Only the third movement, *Games*, with its seldom-used (for beginning bands) rhythmic base of dotted half note as the beat (in 3/4 time) should require extra teaching time. This, however, should not be considered an insurmountable task at the Grade I level. Though much of the scoring is blocked, a fair number of independent lines can be found throughout.

Lawrence Weiner: *Introspection*
Grade III 4:30 European American Music

This piece deals with symphonic legato sonority and emphasizes the rich timbre resources of the band. Following a smooth, rather lush beginning, the piece gives way to a more punctual, disjunct writing. The harmonic warmth of quartal harmony and mixture of quasi-modal tonality with major gives the music its unity and aesthetic growth. The extremely sensitive nature gives the younger performer the opportunity to be musically expressive.

Clifton Williams: *Variation Overture*
Grade III 6:00 Ludwig Music Publishing

Theme and variations form the framework of this concert overture; variation occurs through the presentation of the slightly altered theme in four distinct settings: waltz, lyric, fanfare, and march styles. This overture is an excellent vehicle for the introduction of theme and variation form. The theme is simple and diatonic in nature, allowing the young student to identify it quickly in each of its settings. This is excellent writing for the young band.

Joe Wood: *Catacombs of Rome*
Grade II 2:30 TRN Music

This *fuga di chiesa* is logically conceived, musically appealing, and technically simple enough for the needs of younger musicians. The ensemble will be challenged to produce a legato style and maintain consistent tempo and independence for each section. This music could serve well as a first experience in fugal form, leading of to more advanced fugues; and, as an aid to this study, the *Catacombs* is a must for younger musicians.

Donald Young: *Theme for Phoenix*
Grade III 3:30 Donald Young, manuscript

Manuscript works can open up a new source of interesting literature for young players. *Theme for Phoenix* is similar to much published band music in that it is monothematic, cast in a *slow, fast, slow* mold, and uses some of the rhythmic and melodic patterns that have become familiar in recent band music. It is well written, however, and will make a special addition to a concert program. There are no unusual technical problems in this piece.

PART II: CONCERT MARCHES FOR YOUNG BAND

Beethoven/John Kinyon: *Turkish March*
Grade I   2:45   Alfred Publishing

This straightforward and charming work is suitable for any young band. The woodwinds play a lightly articulated and crisp melody, while the brasses have a less technical harmonic part. Exposure to Classical style as presented here can broaden the musicianship of younger players. This score is a must for Grade I young bands.

James Brush: *Ides of March*
Grade II   2:45   Summy-Birchard

Here is an excellent concert march filled with interesting harmonies, lyrical melodies, and a traditional rhythmic structure. No surprises or pitfalls await the players in this score. This is a splendid march for the advancing Grade II ensemble.

John Cacavas: *Burnished Brass*
Grade III   2:30   Carl Fischer

Junior high school band conductors have programmed this piece so often that it is recognized as a standard in the march repertoire. This energetic 6/8-time march has particularly good woodwind writing, especially in the warm, legato trio section, although generally it is the brass that are dominant. Key relationships, technical aspects, and range considerations make this work both educationally useful and musically appealing.

Rosario Carcione: *Liberty March*
Grade III   3:20   Belwin-Mills Publishing

This flashy concert march has important staccato and accent marks; close attention to the articulation is vital to the effectiveness of the work. The lyrical trio features the baritones. The final strain has woodwind flourishes with full brass sonorities, bringing the work to a dramatic and musical conclusion.

John Cheetham: *March With Flourishes*
Grade III   2:30   TRN Music

Slight variation in the traditional march form and substantial changes in melodic, harmonic, and rhythmic elements are trademarks of this very unusual contemporary march. This work is suitable for groups that are well developed technically and stylistically, and are mature enough to appreciate a rather sophisticated approach to an old form. It is a wonderful addition to the concert march repertoire for the junior high school band.

Lloyd Conley: *Mighty Mac*
Grade II   2:30   Studio P/R

Mighty Mac is characteristic of everything that one loves to hear in a concert march. This singable, 2/2 march has genuine warmth; most certainly, younger musicians will enjoy it. Since key centers of Bb and Eb require a lesser technique, other factors such as style and melodic contour become the major performance issues.

Patrick Conway/Floyd Werle:
The Observing Visitor March
Grade III   6:00   TRN Music

Brilliant trumpet flourishes and trombone melodies make this march an excellent choice for a young band with a virtuosic brass section. This piece sparkles from start to finish, for it is filled with sharp dynamic contrasts and beautiful lyrical melodies over articulated accompaniments and fanfares. The percussion parts are secondary, but add rhythmic clarity and precision. This is a brilliant march.

James Curnow: *Journey to Centaurus*
Grade III   2:30   TRN Music

This concisely written march in simple *ABA* form is well suited to the playing skills of young musicians. After an opening flurry, the work fits together with a weaving of inner lines and musically effective melodic material. The frequent changes between triplet and duplet divisions of the beat will provide a means for younger players to learn this important aspect of rhythm. The overall effect of this march is of rich flavors, and the musical impact upon the players should be positive.

M.L. Daniels: *Tower*
Grade II   3:30   TRN Music

This concert march features well-conceived melodic material in a totally conventional harmonic and rhythmic context. The scoring is safe as well, with the melody, harmony, counter-melody, and bass line heavily doubled. There is need for crisp, muted articulations from the cornets, but other technical demands are modest. This is a "warm" concert march which should appeal to the musical taste of all concerned.

Frank Erickson: *Concord March*
Grade II   2:45   Summit Publications

Only a brief passage in G Major raises the difficulty of this little march above a Grade I. With a clear-cut form, change of key and carefully controlled melodic construction, it presents ample learning opportunities for very young bands. Almost all players are assigned melodic parts, avoiding the accompanying roles oftentimes found in pieces of this genre.

Frank Erickson: *Lyric March*
Grade II 3:30 Summit Publications

This is a wonderful concert march with an immediate appeal to both player and listener. There is a very real lyrical and melodic strength in this march. With the exception of a four measure introduction, the march is "straightforward." Key centers of Eb and Ab should present limited technical challenges to the players.

Julius Fucik/Frederick Fennell:
Florentiner March (Grande Marcia Italiana)
Grade III 5:45 Carl Fischer

This is an *operatic* style march that demands nuance and a stylistic understanding; a mature Grade III band or wind ensemble may increase its sensitivity of playing by studying this work. Controlled, crisp, precise playing is required from the entire ensemble at all times, else the needed clarity will be lost. Fortunately, articulations are very clearly and carefully marked in the score, thereby giving students initial stylistic direction. Particularly developed playing is needed from the trombones and baritones, as they often carry the melody in a soli capacity. There is much to be gained through playing this music; it represents a great and continuing tradition in American band performance.

Richard Franko Goldman: *The Foundation*
Grade III 3:30 Mercury Music

The officers and directors of the Guggenheim Foundation are the dedicatees of this spirited march by one of the most influential men in American band music. Although set in the standard march format and constructed within conservative stylistic principles, it will demand very careful preparation by even the finest of young bands. Each player must be articulate and produce a confident and controlled sound. The conductor will need to spend time in rehearsal teaching the many different articulations that are often found juxtaposed in the score. The only technical demand past Grade III is a high first trumpet part. This march, with its historical importance in the repertoire, is quality fare for concert bands.

Ralph Hale: *Greenway March*
Grade I 1:30 TRN Music

Although short in duration, this rather straightforward march contains an introduction, first and second strain, and a trio. The rhythmic base is 2/4 throughout, and young players should have little difficulty with either rhythmic or technical aspects. The scoring is quite safe for young bands, with divisi parts found only in the clarinet, trumpet, and trombone. This is an exceptional march for those very early stages of concert performance.

Gustav Holst/Jim Curnow:
Moorside March: From A Moorside Suite
Grade III 2:20 R. Smith and Co. Ltd.

This march is the third movement of Holst's "Moorside Suite," written in 1928 as a brass band contest piece. This edition, although shorter in duration than the earlier one by Gordon Jacon, retains the original key centers of B flat, D flat, B flat, thereby giving the music the same rich sonic effectiveness. This edition requires that the younger musician still play with contrasting legato, staccato, and marcato style. Here is an opportunity for younger players to perform Holst: Even though performance requirements are demanding, endurance problems associated with this music are lessened considerably by its under three minute duration.

George Kenny: *Band of Gold*
Grade III 3:30 C.L. Barnhouse

This well-designed, dynamic march is thoroughly traditional as to form, harmonic progression, and style, which features heavy accents and full sonorities.

John Kinyon: *Ocala March*
Grade I 1:30 Alfred Publishing

Young players will find great satisfaction in this simple, straightforward march. This piece presents almost no technical difficulties, except for a short obbligato in the first clarinet. Traditional march form can be taught and experienced through *Ocala*, as well as subito dynamic changes and light, crisp articulation. Percussion parts contain no rolls or flams, although varied sixteenth note patterns occur throughout.

John N. Klohr: *The Billboard March*
Grade III 2:35 Carl Fischer

The name of John N. Klohr (b. 1869), like so many of our nation's early march composers, may be all but forgotten, except when one hears the trio, "Show-Biz,Inc.," of this march. This edition, prepared by the ever skillful Frederick Fennell, is very clear in its musical intentions. Rhythmic notational clarity, articulations, dynamics, and percussion writing are excellent, leaving the skillful conductor and musicians the challenge of placing the "spirit" and "taste" into the music. Although the key centers of E flat and A flat will allow the technique to develop, the major factor in this march is the brisk tempo of half note equals 140.

William Latham: *Brighton Beach*
Grade III   3:15   Summy-Birchard

This beautifully written march is one of the classics of the repertoire. Its character ranges from sounds of fanfare, to lightly articulated woodwind flourishes, to a trio with a sonorous "British" sound. This is a march of special worth, a challenging musical adventure for only the mature and musically proficient young wind band.

William Latham: *March Five*
Grade III   3:30   C.L. Barnhouse

Here is a march that adeptly mixes jazz, traditional, and rock idiom so as to form a skillfully-scored "crossover" piece. There are optional electric guitar and electric bass parts. Percussion is active and interesting.

Florencio Ledesma and **Rafael Oropesa:** *Domingo Ortega*
Grade III   2:00   TRN Music

The *paso doble* is most often "too technical" for younger bands, but the present arrangement is well within the grasp of younger players. The band is required to play with intelligent technique and delicate, crisp articulation, but the heart of this music is in its *paso doble* style. Fortunately, an excellent set of program notes and rehearsal suggestions will help conductor and players realize this style.

James Lewallen: *March II*
Grade II   2:30   Studio P/R

A 6/8 march is usually a challenge to young players; this 6/8 march will be especially challenging because of chromatic alterations that occur as the music passes through various keys. The march is in five sections, and is excellent for concert use and as 6/8 teaching material.

Mozart/Ross Hastings: *March of the Offstage Army*
Grade II   2:20   Bourne Publishing

Taken from *Cosi fan tutti*, Hastings' scoring largely parallels the original. Except for the woodwind trills, which must be neatly executed to sound idiomatic, the work is not technically difficult. The fundamental challenge is the striving for an elegance of interpretation.

Eric Osterling: *Thundercrest*
Grade III   2:30   Carl Fischer

This lively 6/8 concert march is a longtime favorite of junior high conductors. From its driving rhythmical unisons to its more tender melodies, this march is in all ways enjoyable. Modulations from Eb major to Db major will present some technical challenge; these notwithstanding, the music should be learned fairly quickly.

Richard Otto: *Antares*
Grade III   2:30   Carl Fischer

This 6/8 concert march incorporates a lyrical quality with precise tonguing styles in a most interesting and challenging harmonic fabric – F, G, Ab, and Eb major. The major charm is the slippery, "collegiate" melody as it wends its chromatic way.

James Ployhar: *March of the Irish Guard*
Grade I   2:30   Carl Fischer

Old Irish melodies tend to be of exceptional quality, and this 4/4 tune has a strong character and grace. A *same tempo* 6/8 middle section (the 4/4 section quarter note equals the 6/8 section dotted half note) will provide a reasonable challenge to young players. The arrangement is solid and safe, and in always attractively written. It is also useful as an easy Grade II.

James Ployhar: *Sultan's Saber*
Grade I   2:20   Belwin-Mills Publishing

This rather simple, straightforward and somewhat exotic-sounding march is a delightful piece for the very early stages of ensemble performance. The writing is safe, practical, and logical for those first rehearsals. Clarinets do not perform above the break; other instruments are written within playable ranges. Frequent solo passages by percussionists also provide interest, as does the OOM-pah-pah-pah "Sultan" ostinato in drums with tambourine accompaniment. This music will aid young bands in experiencing a feeling of secure togetherness, and provide the audience with a "different" sounding concert work.

William Rhoads: *Marche de Provencal*
Grade II   3:00   TRN Music

This march is straight from the European town band tradition, and its presence in the march repertoire is important. There are no unusual technical demands for the strong Grade II ensemble. Placed on a program with marches of other styles, or with other pieces of its genre, this is music with appeal.

William Schaefer: *Three French Marches*
Grade III   9:10   Alphonse Leduc

This edition of marches comes from three historic periods of French history: the revolution, the court of Henry IV, and the Napoleonic Wars. The marches are contrasting, and present little performance difficulty, except for the execution of correct musical style. The first march has a rather lively tempo and dotted rhythms; the second is slower, with woodwind sections providing relief from the larger tutti sections; the third, by Louis Jadin, is more courtly than the other two. This music is noteworthy in itself, but the historical value adds to the teaching and performance usefulness of this edition.

Claude T. Smith: *March Spiritoso*
Grade III 2:50 Wingert-Jones Music

Here is a concert march filled with melodic lyricism, rhythmic vitality, and vivid sonorities. Musical depth is attained through the composer's use of three themes, presented successively and later fused to form a musical and grandiose ending. Players will learn to perform triplet figures in 2/2 time in this march.

John Philip Sousa: *Marches (various)*

Due to the efforts of conductors such as Keith Brion, the march music of Sousa is experiencing a much-deserved renaissance. Careful editions of many of his best marches have been prepared not only by Brion, but by Frederick Fennell, Harold Gore, and Donald Hunsberger as well. These critical editions take particular care in adding dynamics, articulations, and percussion parts that are believed to have been used by Sousa, although never before notated.

Since most of Sousa's marches are too difficult for even Grade III bands, the following marches, selected by the author and Dr. Donald S. George, Director of Bands of the University of Wisconsin–Eau Claire, are of particular interest to the conductor of young bands. They are all approachable by technically secure Grade III bands.

The Beau Ideal, ed. Gore
Grade III 3:10 Alfred Publishing
King Cotton, ed. Fennell
Grade III 2:40 John Church
Liberty Bell, ed. Brion
Grade III 3:10 Hal Leonard
The Loyal Legion, ed. Hunsberger
Grade III 2:45 Ludwig Publishing
On The Tramp, ed. Gore
Grade III 1:55 Bourne Publishing
Sound Off, orig. ed.
Grade III 3:00 Carl Fischer
Riders For The Flag, ed. Fennell
Grade III 2:20 Sam Fox
The Washington Post, ed. Fennell
Grade III 3:00 Carl Fischer

Mike Story: *A Jubilant March*
Grade II 3:00 Studio P/R

This sparkling march is all that one would want for younger musicians: A brilliant introduction, melodic first and second strains, and legato warmth are to be found. Expected march style, brief syncopation figures, and interesting parts for all are found in this delightful march.

Edgar Thiessen: *KMB March*
Grade III 2:30 Belwin-Mills Publishing

This is a standard, well-written march that is useful programmatically when foot-tapping music is required. The march was written for the *Kiel Municipal Band* of Kiel, Wisconsin. Its form is traditional, with two sections based on punctuated melodic lines and a trio with augmented rhythmic values with a contrasting melodic tenor part. The percussion parts heighten the climaxes, but otherwise provide only an accompaniment to the wind parts.

Norman Ward: *Splashdown!*
Grade I 1:20 Kendor Music

Very traditional in style, *Splashdown!* is a good vehicle for introduction of march style to more advanced Grade level I players. There are some syncopations in the accompaniment figures, but nothing that cannot be easily assimilated by young players. The melody has a traditional "football-field" feel to it.

Ken Whitcomb: *County Fair*
Grade III 2:45 Heritage Music Press

Colorful writing for woodwinds and brass highlights this flashy, well-conceived concert march. The design is quite standard for marches of this genre (*Introduction/A/B/Trio/Coda*) and its musical material should be appealing to players. Chromatic runs, woodwind obbligatos, flowing melodies, and short brass flourishes are present. Woodwinds have quite active, technical parts. By all measures, the piece should be appealing to all and well worth effort in rehearsal.

Ken Whitcomb: *Fireball*
Grade II 2:45 C.L. Barnhouse

This is not a straightforward march at all: The key center is c minor, with frequent use of the flatted sixth that gives the march a jazzy flavor. The wind and percussion writing is not excessively demanding, and mature Grade II bands should be capable of dealing with its technique. The music is good concert material.

Kenneth Williams/Alfred Reed: *Vilabella*
Grade III 3:44 Sam Fox Publishing

This excellently written and orchestrated concert march possesses all the ingredients one enjoys in marches — woodwind flourishes, brilliantly articulated brass textures, and supportive, tasteful percussion. Key centers of Eb, Ab, C, and Db can provide a major challenge. However, ranges and rhythms are reasonable, making the music more manageable by younger bands.

Charles Wiley: *Earl's March*
Grade III   2:30   TRN Music

   This traditional march setting includes some interesting, subtle deviations from conventional writing. A "nursery-tune" derivation forms the melodic content of the trio. The scoring is often brilliant, and the ebb and flow of line and dynamic together produce a very musical result. Ranges and technical aspects are well-suited to younger musicians; only the trumpets and horns will find challenges with upper register playing.

Charles Wiley: *Lowlands March*
Grade III   3:00   TRN Music

   Based upon two Dutch folk songs and the Royal Dutch National Anthem, this march is rich in sound and texture. Technical passages for woodwinds and trumpets will present an adequate challenge for these players. Smooth articulation will be the major problem if the aesthetic character of the music is to live. Tasteful percussion writing for bells, chimes, drums, and timpani add a musical dimension to this already attractive piece. This is a march rich in sound, and ideally dignified and grand.

PART III: CONCERT/FESTIVAL WORKS FOR YOUNG WIND ENSEMBLE

Anthony Baines: *Nine Easy Pieces for Wind Groups*
Grade II   11:00   Oxford University Press
2 ob./3 cl. or trp./bn. or trb./2 hn.

These nine brief wind octets from the 17th and 18th century form a good collection of period music. The collection includes two French marches, a Swiss waltz, a setting of Greensleeves, a work of Schubert (Op. 94, No. 6), and others. Although the bulk of the tunes are Grade II, some of them are simple and brief enough to be playable by better Grade I bands. Ranges, key signatures, and scoring requirements are within the grasp of young players.

Raymond Birch/Timothy Broege: *Blue Goose Rag*
Grade III   2:30   Manhattan Beach Music
Symphonic Wind Ensemble

The continuing popularity of the "Roaring Twenties" style and the music of Scott Joplin in particular has yielded a number of period pieces for instrumental combinations. Most, however, are beyond the reach of younger players. This clever arrangement is not only very accessible to such players, but it has a real vitality. The transparent nature of ragtime music requires one player per part in this edition.

Joel Blahnik: *Six Ceremonial Fanfares*
Grade III   00:08 to 00:36   E.C. Kerby
picc.-fl./cls./a. sax./t. sax./corn./hns./trb./bar./tu./perc.

These fanfares provide a fine resource for concert openers. Each of the six fanfares is dramatic and filled with energy. Brass ranges, especially in the first cornet (to high c), and trumpet (also to high c) will require strength. Although quite short in length, these fanfares are excellent for concert use.

Walter Hartley: *Prologue and March from 'Ballet Music'*
Grade III   2:30   FEMA Music Publications
Symphonic Wind Ensemble

For conductors familiar with Walter Hartley's wind band music, this piece is a welcome addition to the young wind ensemble/band repertoire. Written in 1949 for orchestra and transcribed for band in 1960, the music is transparent, linearly clear, yet delicate. Important across-the-bar syncopation figures play a primary role in this music. The piece calls for standard instrumentation, but 2 bassoons, 4 horns, and string bass are absolute essentials. The music is fresh and uncluttered.

Gordon Jacob: *Giles Farnaby Suite*
Grade III   19:00   Boosey & Hawkes
Symphonic Wind Ensemble

To wind conductors, the name Gordon Jacob is synonymous with musical craft. This suite of eleven varied works from the *Fitzwilliam Virginal Book* is no exception. As a piece in its entirety, and in selected movements, the music is a masterwork for younger players. Ranges, key signatures, and technical requirements are well-designed, and with careful preparation technical requirements should be easily handled, although a marked fluency of technique, particularly in the woodwinds, is essential in some movements. Like much early keyboard music transcribed for winds, one player per part will give the music a more transparent and clear performance.

G.S. McPeek, arr.: *Album of Classical Pieces*
Grade III   7:00   G. Schirmer

This is a collection of seven songs, skillfully arranged so that each can be performed by four instruments taken at random from each one of each of four groups listed here: Group 1—flute, oboe, clarinet; Group 2—flute, oboe, clarinet, alto sax, alto clarinet; Group 3—bassoon, clarinet, alto clarinet, bass clarinet, alto sax, tenor sax; Group 4—bassoon, bass clarinet. Musically there is real treasure in this collection. Conductors who are gearing their students toward chamber wind playing will find this music idiomatic of the time, historically worthwhile, and challenging. The diversity provided by the scoring gives the conductor a virtually endless array of combinations for performance. In the total playing experience of young musicians, this music is a must.

David Moritz Michael/Harry H. Hall, ed.
Parthia II
Grade III   15:00   Boosey & Hawkes
fl./2 cl./bn./2 hn.

Among the fourteen *Parthias* of David Moritz Michael (1751-1827), nos. II, IV, and VI are quite surprisingly within the playing capabilities of younger musicians. *Parthia II* offers the flute the opportunity to join the more traditional chamber ensemble setting of clarinets, bassoons, and horns. Intelligent technique and stylistic performance are essential to all players, but predominantly to the flute and clarinets. This five-movement work is a must for the serious-minded conductor.

David Moritz Michael/Harry H. Hall, ed.:
Parthia IV
GradeIII   14:00   Boosey & Hawkes

2 cl./2 bn./2 hn.

The rhythmic structure of this sextet and the use of simple melodies provide young players with the opportunity to engage in the performance of good chamber music. The development of a sensitive, Mozartian playing style and a musical independence are benefits of studying this music.

David Moritz Michael/Donald M. McCorkle, ed.
Parthia VI
Grade III 12:00 Boosey & Hawkes
2 cl./2 bn./2 hn.

McCorkle has called the *Parthia VI* one of the best of the fourteen *Parthias*. It is a four-movement sonata form of the style typical of Viennese classical woodwind music after 1790. The piece demands a fluent and musical technique from the first clarinet and first bassoon. The other parts, however, serve as an accompaniment and therefore present fewer technical challenges. This edition, like Michael's other *Parthias* are absolute cornerstones in the chamber music program.

Mozart/Francis Caviani: *Menuetto Allegretto*
Grade III 3:30 Kendor Music
Symphonic Wind Ensemble

This Mozart arrangement comes from the *Gran Partita*, K. 361, which was written for thirteen wind instruments in 1781. The conductor has ample opportunity to develop in his players a sense of the Classical style with its demands for control, grace, delicacy, and transparency. Conductors will greatly enhance the music by utilizing a smaller wind ensemble extracted from the full band. Playing this piece is a fine opportunity for students to experience music written for wind instruments in situations where they might not be able to find the necessary oboes, bassoons, and horns to perform Mozart's original orchestration.

Mozart/David Schanke: *March Viennese*
Grade III 3:30 Music Arts Publishing
Symphonic Wind Ensemble

Although this arrangement is scored for full band, it is perhaps better suited for a wind group of lesser size. Because of the genre, the primary task of this piece will be controlled playing; the music does not present technical or instrumental ensemble problems. Listening to short excerpts of the many professional recordings of Mozart's wind music will greatly enhance the stylistic appreciation. This is a most worthwhile work for advanced players "extracted" from the full band.

Peter Philips: *Gothic Suite*
Grade III 7:30 Oxford University Press

This is a setting of five medieval songs, beginning with a brief, lyric fanfare. Demands of range and technique are not excessive, although the piece requires rather intelligent technique and musicianship from all players. The composition possesses a wealth of tonal concepts and stylistic practices; there is considerable variety among the movements, both as to tempo and texture. Though scored for band, this work may indeed be better suited to one player per part. This unusual work is quite off the well-traveled path and worth more than a look.

Erik Satie/Kenneth Megan: *Three Gymnopedies*
Grade III 5:00 E.C. Schirmer Music
2 fl./2 ob./solo cl./2 cl./bn./
2 hn./2 perc./guitar/harp/piano/str. bs.

This piece is taken from Satie's work for piano of the same name. Key centers of D and C major will likely cause the greatest performance challenge for young players. The instrumentation is very interesting, emphasizing the light and transparent sounds associated with Satie's music. The work itself consists of three connected sections, woven around the solo clarinet, while the other voices serve in a basic accompanying role.

Carl Maria von Weber/Bram Wiggins:
Five German Dances
Grade III 8:00 Oxford University Press
Symphonic Wind Ensemble (without sax.)

Originally written for piano, these dances are beautifully scored for wind ensemble. Like the *Five Waltzes* of von Weber/Wiggins, these pieces are in all ways musically rich, calling for the very best of skilled musicianship. This music is simply charming, easy to listen to and deserving of performance by players who can play its delicate musical fabric. Where serious wind chamber music is valued, this work should appear on the program for young musicians.

Carl Maria von Weber/Bram Wiggins:
Five Waltzes
Grade III 8:00 Oxford University Press
Symphonic Wind Ensemble (without sax.)

This attractive collection of waltzes was originally written for piano, and has been skillfully transcribed by one of the band world's most respected arrangers, Bram Wiggins. The instrumentation is clearly for wind ensemble, calling for one player per part, and omitting the entire saxophone family. These waltzes are contrasting, but all beg for the utmost in musical style and spirit. This piece will require the very best efforts from the finest players of the ensemble. As young wind ensemble music, this ranks as cornerstone repertoire.

James Walker: *Encore for Winds*
Grade III 2:30 G. Schirmer
2 fl./2 ob./2 bn./2 cl./2 trp./2 hn.

The distinguishing features of this classical scherzo are rapid speed in 3/4 meter, a vigorous rhythmic excitement, and a truly engaging character of bustling humor. It will require skillful players to bring these characteristics to life. Technically, the music lies very well for all the instruments; the major challenge will be the chromatic alterations and the often difficult syncopations.

ADDRESSES

Alfred Publishing Company, Inc.
15335 Morrison Street
Sherman Oaks, CA 91403

Allaire Music Publishing
93 Gooseneck Point Road
Oceanport, NJ 07757

C.L. Barnhouse Company
110 B. Avenue East
Oskaloosa, IA 52577

Belwin-Mills Publishing Corp.
U.S. distributor: Columbia Pictures

Joel Blahnik
Spring Road
Fish Creek, WI 54212

Joseph Boonin, Inc.
U.S. distributor: European American

Boosey & Hawkes, Inc.
200 Smith Street
Farmingdale, NY 11735

Boston Music Company
116 Boylston Street
Boston, MA 02116

Bourne Publishing Company
437 Fifth Avenue
New York, NY 10036

Timothy Broege
93 Gooseneck Point Road
Oceanport, NJ 07757

Canyon Press
Box 1235
Cincinnatti, OH 45201

The John Church Co.
U.S. distributor: Presser

Chappell & Company, Inc.
810 Seventh Avenue
New York, NY 10019

J. Christopher Music Co.
U.S. Distributor: European American

Franco Colombo Publications
U.S. Distributor: Belwin-Mills (see Colombia)

Columbia Pictures Publications
P.O. Box 4340
Hialeah, FL 33014

Elkan-Vogel Co., Inc.
U.S. Distributor: Theodore Presser

European American Dist. Corp.
P.O. Box 850
Valley Forge, PA 19482

FEMA Music Publications
P.O. Box 395
Naperville, IL 60540

Carl Fischer, Inc.
62 Cooper Square
New York, NY 10003

Sam Fox Publishing Co.
U.S. Distributor: Plymouth

G.I.A. Publications
7404 South Mason Avenue
Chicago, IL 60638

David Gillingham
Central Michigan University
Department of Music
Mt. Pleasant, MI 48859

Heritage Music Press
U.S. Distributor: Lorenz

Jenson Publications, Inc.
2880 South 171st Street
New Berlin, WI 53151

Kendor Music, Inc.
P.O. Box 278
Delevan, NY 14042

E.C. Kirby, Ltd.
198 Davenport Road
Toronto, Canada M5R 1J2

Neil A. Kjos Music Company
4382 Jutland Drive
San Diego, CA 92117

Alphonnse Leduc
U.S. distributor: Presser
(175, rue Saint-Honore
Paris, France)

Hal Leonard Publishing Corp.
8112 West Bluemound Road
Milwuakee, WI 53123

Ludwig Music Publishing Company
557-67 East 140th Street
Cleveland, OH 44110

Manhattan Beach Music
1595 East 46th Street
Brooklyn, NY 11234

Edward B. Marks Music Corp.
U.S. distributor: Hal Leonard

MCA Music
U.S. Distributor: Hal Leonard

Mercury Music
U.S. Distributor: Presser

Merion Publishers
U.S. Distributor: Presser

Donal Michalsky manuscript
care of: Eugene Corporon
School of Music
Michigan State University
East Lansing, MI 48824

Music Arts Publishing Co.
P.O. Box 327
Ripon, WI 54971

Oxford University Press
200 Madison Avenue
New York, NY 10016

Peer International
U.S. Distributor: Peer-Southern

Peer-Southern Organization
1740 Broadway
New York, NY 10019

C.F. Peters Corp.
373 Park Avenue South
New York, NY 10016

Theodore Presser Co.
Presser Place
Bryn Mawr, PA 19010

Pro Art Publications, Inc.
U.S. Distributor: Belwin-Mills (see Colombia)

Willis Schaefer
1244 Valley View Rd.
Glendale, CA 91202

E.C. Schirmer Music Company
112 South Street
Boston, MA 02111

G. Schirmer, Inc.
866 Third Avenue
New York, NY 10022

Peter Schmalz
1303 Faust Avenue
Oshkosh, WI 54901

Shawnee Press, Inc.
Delaware Water Gap, PA 18327

R. Smith & Co., Ltd.
U.S. Distributor: Jenson

Southern Music Co.
1100 Broadway
San Antonio, TX 78206

Thomas Stone
521 Briar Place, Ap't. 406
Chicago, IL 60657

Studio P/R, Inc.
U.S. Distributor: Columbia

Summitt Publications
U.S. Distributor: Belwin-Mills (see Colombia)

Summy-Birchard Co.
U.S. Distributor: Birch Tree

TOA Music International Co.
U.S. distributor: Hal Leonard
(KAGURAZAKA 6-30,
Shin-Juku-Ku,
Tokyo 162, Japan)

TRN Music
P.O. Box 1076
Ruidoso, NM 88345

Warner Bros. Music
U.S. Distributor: Jenson

Wingert-Jones Music, Inc.
2026 Broadway
Kansas City, MO 64141

Donald Young
3634 Douglas Avenue, No. 704
Racine, WI 53402

TITLE INDEX

ARRANGER/EDITOR INDEX

This book has been digitally phototypeset in Paladium and *Paladium Italic* using 10 point type on 11¾ points leading
Book design by Bob Margolis
Cover design by Neil Ruddy